Microsoft Project

Bible

Microsoft Project

Bible

By

Jason Taylor

Microsoft Project Bible

Copyright © 2024 Jason Taylor

All rights reserved. This book or any portion thereof may not be reproduced or used in any manner whatsoever without the express written permission of the writer except for the use of brief quotations in a book review.

Jason Taylor

TABLE OF CONTENTS

Chapter One 15
    Investigate The Project User Interface 15
    Use The Backstage View To Manage Files And Configure Settings 24

Chapter Two 28
    Templates 28
    Templates In Your Company 28
    How To Start A New Project With A Blank Plan 29
    How To Develop A New Plan Using Data In A Different File Format, Another Plan, Or A Template 29
    To Start A Project 30
    To Save A Project 30
    Using An Existing Plan As A Template 30
    How To Change Between Viewpoints 33
    How To Modify A View's Timescale 33
    How To Show A Split View (Combination) 34
    How To Make The Timeline View Visible Or Invisible 34
    Utilize Reports To Assess The Progress Of A Project ... 35
    To Develop A Fresh Strategy 37
    To Determine (Or Modify) The Commencement Date Of The Plan 37
    How To Save The New Project 38
    How To Choose The Project Schedule 42
    How To Designate A Particular Date As Nonworking .. 42
    How To Establish A Regular Nonworking Period 42

How To Arrange A Special Work Week 43
How To Add The Other Properties And The Project Title
.... 44
How To Access The Attributes Of A Plan 44
Make Tasks 47
To Input Task Names 49
To Add A New Task To A List Of Tasks 49
To Remove A Task 49
Focus Of Project Management 50
Advice 53

Chapter Three 56
Entering A Milestone Task 56
How To Designate A Task As A Milestone, Regardless Of Its Duration 56
How To Add A New Summary Task To A List Of Tasks
.... 58
Connect Tasks To Establish Dependencies 59
How To Connect Tasks 61
How To Disconnect Tasks 63
How To Change The Manual Scheduling Of Specific Tasks Or The Full Plan To An Automated One 64
How To Convert The Existing Open Plan's Work Scheduling From Manual To Automatic 65
How To Modify The Project's Default Scheduling Mode For All New Tasks 66
How To Show The Task For The Project Summary 69
How To Include A Message In A Task 71

How To Give A Task A Hyperlink 71

Chapter Four 73

Make Tasks 73

How To Remove A Resource 92

Advice 94

How To Input A Resource's Standard Rate 97

How To Input A Resource's Overtime Rate 98

How To Input A Resource's Cost Per Use 98

Chapter Five 101

Work Resource 101

How To Change The Default Working Week Days And
Timings For A Resource 102

How To Give A Resource A Different Base Calendar . 104

Cost Resources For Setup 104

Filling Out The Resource Information Dialog Box With
A Resource Note 107

Using The Resource Form To Add A Note For A
Resource 107

To Assign A Work Resource To A Task 108

Using The Task Form View To Examine Or Modify
Assignment Details 110

Control Work When Adding Or Withdrawing Resource
Assignments 110

How To Alter The Schedule Outcome When A Task's
Resource Is Removed 115

How To Oversee The Scheduling Of An Effort-Driven
Activity Or Tasks 116

- Assign Tasks To Cost Resources 116
- To Allocate A Task's Cost Resource 117
- How To Verify The Expenses For Each Task In The Plan 119
- To Determine The Expenses Of Each Resource In The Plan 119
- How To View Resource Allocation And Additional Information Organized By Task 120
- How To View Task Assignments And Additional Information Categorized By Resource 120

Chapter Six 121

- Customize Reports, Add Tasks To A Timeline View, And Alter A Gantt Chart View 121
- How To Give Gantt Bars A Gantt Chart Appearance .. 127
- How To Format A Unique Gantt Chart Form 128
- How To Get Rid Of Every Formatting That Has Been Put On A Cell 129
- How To Format A Range Of Cells Or A Single Cell ... 132
- How To Get Rid Of Every Formatting That Has Been Put On A Cell 132
- How To Modify The Timeline In A Gantt Chart View 133
- How To Include Already-Completed Tasks In A Timeline View 134
- How To Show A Report 134
- How To Add A Style To A Report's Chart 134
- How To Give A Table In A Report A Style 135

Chapter Seven 136

How To Replicate A View 137
Print Reports And Views 138
How To Print A View 141
How To Print A Report 141
How To Modify A Report's Page Setup Parameters 142
Monitor Progress: Fundamental Methods 142
Recognize Progress Tracking 143
How To Remove A Baseline That Has Already Been
Saved 149
How To Use The Variance Table To Show Scheduled
And Baseline Values 150
How To Alter The Kind Of Task-To-Task Relationship
.... 151
How To Increase The Lead Time Or Lag Time Between
Related Tasks 152
How To Use Restrictions To Manage The Scheduling Of
Tasks 152
How To Get Rid Of A Task Restriction 162

Chapter Eight 164

How To Divide A Task 164
Adapt Working Hours To Specific Tasks 165
To Assign A Task To A Base Calendar 168
To Utilize Column Headings To Filter Activities Or
Resources 170
How To Make Or Modify A Filter 171
How To Apply A Custom Or Built-In Filter To Activities
Or Resources 174

Using Pre-Installed Or Custom Highlight Filters To Draw Attention To Tasks Or Resources 175

How To Remove The Resources' Or Tasks' Filtering Or Highlighting 175

Make New Tables 176

How To Modify Or Make A Unique Table 177

How To Make A Table Have A Column 180

Make Fresh Views 180

How To Make Or Modify A View 183

Details Of The Filter Plan 186

Make New Tables 187

Make New Views 188

How To Document The Amount Of Work Completed And Left On Each Task 190

How To Document Completed And Unfinished Work For Each Assignment 191

Chapter Nine 197

Focus Of Project Management: Gather Data From Resources 197

Using The Task Usage View To Document Time-Phased Actual Work 199

How To Document Actual Labor That Is Time-Phased In The Resource Usage View 200

Rescheduled Unfinished Work 200

How To Postpone Unfinished Tasks 202

How To Open The Project Statistics Dialog Box 202

How To Determine Which Tasks Have Fallen Behind 203

To Show The Variance Table In The View Of The Task Sheet 205

How To Show The Gantt Chart For Tracking 205

How To Show The Report On Late Or Slipping Tasks 205

Analyze The Costs Of The Task 206

How To View The Plan's Cost And Cumulative Cost Values Over Time, Display The Cash Flow Report 208

How To Show The Cash Flow Report Or Task Cost Overview 210

Analyze The Costs Of Resources 210

How To Display The Cost Table In The Resource Sheet View 213

How To Sort Resources By Cost Amounts 213

How To Display The Cost Table And Cost Information In The Resource Usage View 214

Chapter Ten 215

Format And Print Views: Comprehensive Methods 215

Set Up A Gantt Chart 215

How To Design A New Gantt Chart 222

How To Add Or Modify Text That Is Shown Using A Gantt Chart 224

How To Change The Drawing Precedence Order, Rearrange The Bar Styles 225

Create A Timeline View 225

How To Alter The Text Styles Of The Timeline 229

How To Format An Item In A Timeline Directly 229

- How To Expand The Timeline View By Adding More Timeline Bars (Up To 10) 230
- How To Change The Range Of Dates That A Timeline Bar Is Shown Over 230
- Create A View Of A Network Diagram 231
- How To Make Or Alter A Network Diagram Box Data Template (Node) 237
- How To Change A Particular Task Box (Node) In The Display Of The Network Diagram 238

Chapter Eleven 239

- Create A Calendar View Format 239
- How To Modify Week Height 240

Printing 240

- How To Change The Print Settings 245
- How To Modify View-Specific Settings 245
- How To Alter The Header Or Footer Of A View 245
- How To Create An Xps Or Pdf File 246
- Make A Unique Report 247

How Views And Reporting Compare 249

- How To Produce A New Report 251
- How To Include A Chart In A Report 251
- How To Include A Table In A Report 252
- How To Include A Text Field In A Report 252
- How To Give A Report A Shape 252
- How To Include A Picture In A Report 253
- Personalize A Report's Charts 253

Features For Organizing Data (Filter, Group By, Etc.) 257

How To Alter The Style And Format Of A Chart 259

.... 261

How To Alter The Layout And Design Of A Table 262

Chapter Twelve **264**

Modify The Project 264

How To Duplicate A Component Of Two Designs 268

How To Transfer A Personalized Component To The Global Template 269

How To Stop The Global Template From Automatically Adding Customized Elements 269

Record And Execute Macros 270

How To Capture A Macro 273

How To Remove A Macro 274

Modify Macros 274

How To Make Changes To A Macro 278

Personalize The Quick Access Toolbar And Ribbon ... 278

How To Personalize The Ribbon 282

How To Restore The Ribbon's Original Look 283

Chapter Thirteen **285**

Exchanging Data With Other Programs 285

Pasting Tabular Data Into Project From Another Program 289

How To Open A File In A Different Format 294

Save Project Files In Different Formats 297

Distribute A Resource Pool Among Several Plans 301

Linking A Plan To A Pool Of Resources 307

How To Disconnect A Resource Pool From A Sharer Plan 308

How To Change A Sharer Plan's Read-Only Resource Pool 309

How To Oversee Resource Pool-Connected Sharer Plans 310

How To Adjust The Working Hours For Each Sharer Plan In A Resource Pool 311

Combine Plans 312

How To Show An Inserted Plan's Details 316

How To Show The Aggregated Plan's Project Summary Task 317

Chapter Fourteen 318

Establish Interdependence Between Plans 318

How To Establish Connections Between Two Plans ... 321

How To Establish Cross-Plan Connections Between Plans That Have Been Added To A Consolidated Plan 322

How To Modify A Cross-Project Link's Relationship Type In A Consolidated Plan 322

How To Recognize And Oversee Each Link In A Plan, Including External Predecessors And External Successors 323

Combine Plans 324

Establish Interdependence Between Plans Situation ... 324

A Brief Project Management Course 325

Duration/ Time 329

The Price / Cost 330
Scope / Range 330
Time, Money, And Scope: Control Project Limitations
.... 332

Conclusion...**338**

CHAPTER ONE

INVESTIGATE THE PROJECT USER INTERFACE

Project's Start screen shows up when you launch it. This is where you may rapidly open a recently opened plan, open another plan, or make a new one.

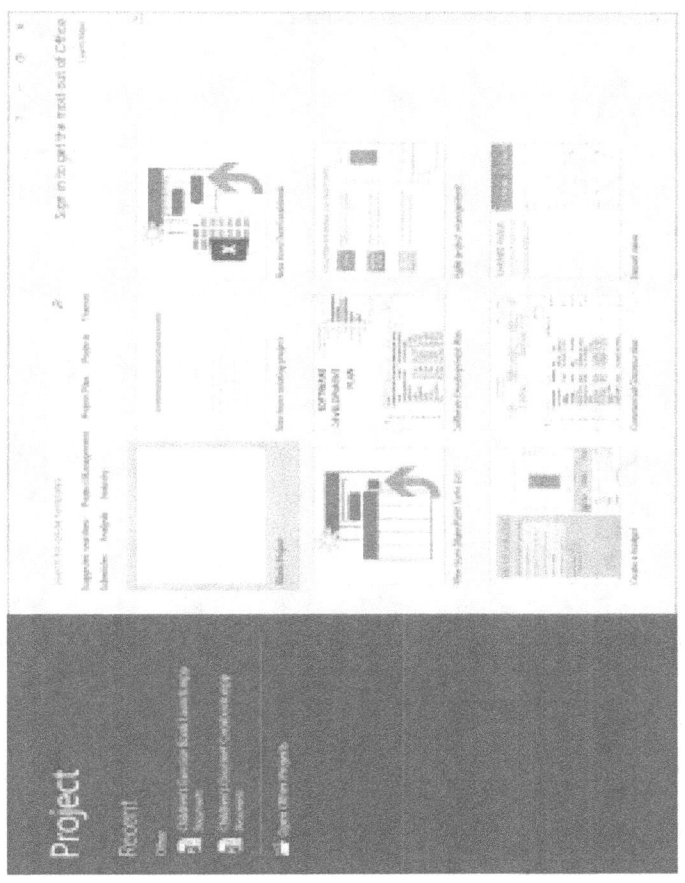

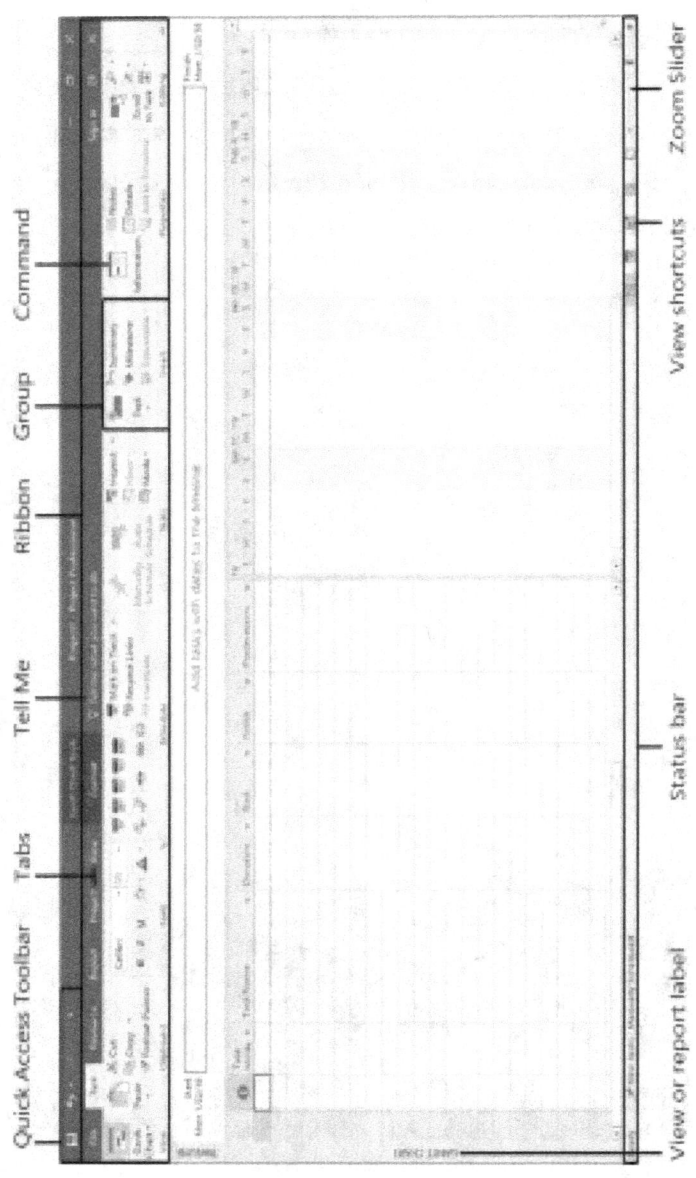

The new plan may be based on an existing plan, a template, or nothing at all. There are choices to access an existing plan or create a new one on the Project Start screen.

If you launch Project without seeing the Start screen, try these steps:

- Select the Options option from the File tab.
- Click General in the Project Options dialog box, then select Show The Start Screen, when This Application Starts under Start Up Options.
- On the Start screen, select the Blank Project option to start a new plan. By doing this, the new plan is created in the Project main interface.

Let's examine the main components of the Project interface: You can add your favorite or most used commands to the Quick Access Toolbar, a part of the UI that can be customized.

To discover a Project command or get assistance with a particular command or functionality, use the **Tell Me box**. The commands you use to carry out actions in Project are located on the ribbon. The ribbon's tabs group Project's main functions and commands into sensible categories. Later in this topic, we go into more detail about the tabs on the

Project ribbon. Groups are sets of commands that are tied to one another. Every tab has several groups.

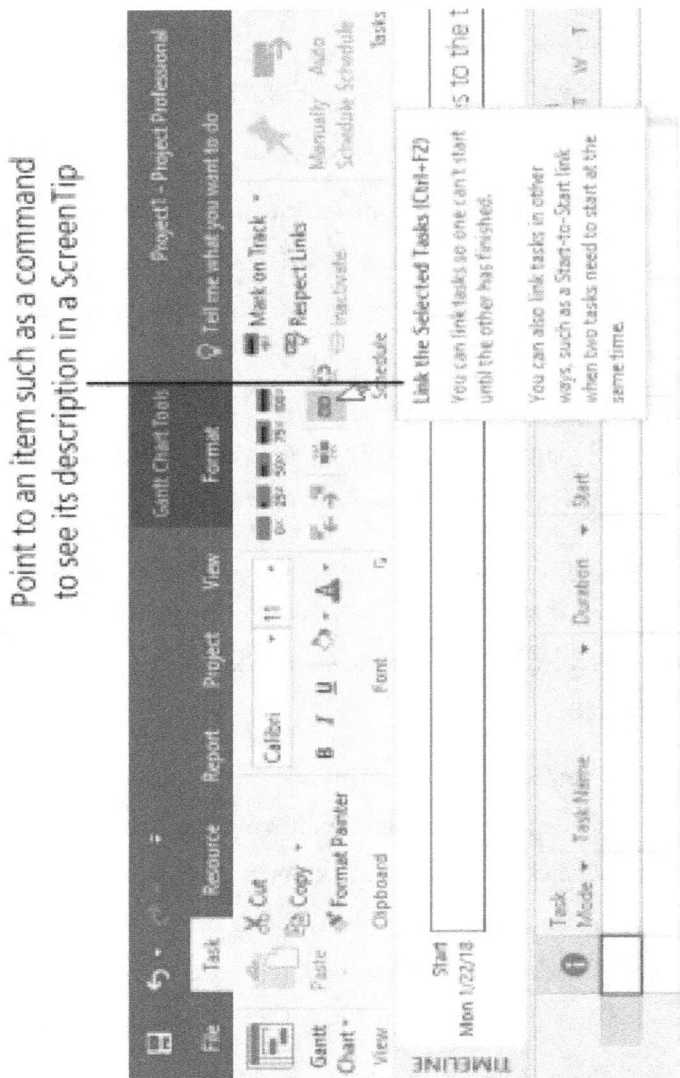

The exact tools you utilize to carry out tasks in Project are called commands. There are multiple commands on each tab. Certain commands, such as Cut on the Task tab, take effect instantly. Some instructions, such as Change Working Time on the Project tab, open a dialog box or otherwise ask you to do something else. Certain instructions can only be used when you are in a specific kind of report or view. ScreenTips are brief explanations of several Project features, including commands and column titles. Pointing to an item will display its ScreenTip.

The primary Project window shows the active view (or report). One view or more views in different panes may be displayed by the project. A split view or combo view is a type of multiple-view display.

On the left side of the active view is the view label, often known as the report label. There are dozens of views in the project, therefore this serves as a helpful reminder of which view is now active. Important information is shown in the status bar, such as whether a filter has been applied to the active view and whether new tasks are scheduled manually or automatically. You can rapidly navigate between recently used views and reports by using view shortcuts. The Zoom Slider allows you to zoom in or out of the report or current display.

When you right-click the majority of objects in a view or report, shortcut menus—also known as context menus or right-click menus—and Mini Toolbars show up. To view the Mini Toolbar and possible shortcut menu actions, right-click on the name of a task or another value.

ADVICE

The following is a good general practice: right-click an item in Project to check what commands are available for it if you're unsure of what to do with it.

Other items, like a **Gantt bar**, can be right-clicked to reveal other commands that are accessible and a different Small Toolbar. Like other Microsoft Office applications, Project makes use of the ribbon-style interface. The tabs and ribbon that extend across the top of the Project window are the most noticeable components of this interface. The commands that pertain to the main Project emphasis areas are appropriately grouped together under these tabs:

- Commands for adding, formatting, and organizing tasks are available on the Task tab.
- To allocate resources to tasks, manage their workloads, and add them to a plan, use the Resource tab.

- You can check reports and compare two plans using the instructions on the Report tab.
- Commands that typically apply to the entire plan, like the one to set the working hours of the plan, are found in the Project tab.
- You may adjust what you see and how that information is presented in the Project window by using the View tab.
- A few examples of tool tabs include the Layout, Design, and Format tabs. When a specific type of item is selected or a specific type of information is shown in the active view or report, a tool tab is displayed. For instance, the Format tool tab's commands apply to both tasks and Gantt Chart elements, such as Gantt bars, when a task view, such as the Gantt Chart view, is displayed. The Format tab's current context is displayed, for instance, above the tab label for Gantt Chart Tools.

The ribbon can be expanded or collapsed by double-clicking a tab label. By clicking the tab label and then choosing the desired command, you can also view a tab that has been collapsed.

Let's examine the tabs in more detail below.

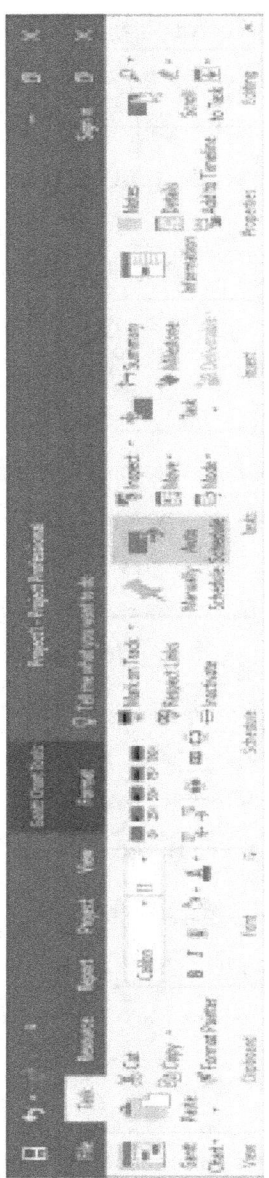

Microsoft Project Bible

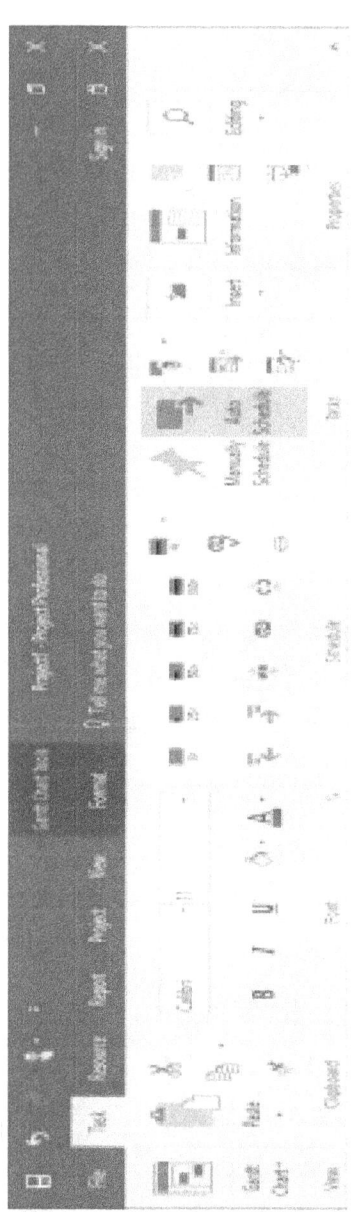

The View, Clipboard, Font, and other groups are located

on the Task tab. The commands on the ribbon look larger and some don't have text labels if you enabled touch input (by

While some commands provide you with more options, others take immediate action. A split button is an example of the second kind of command, which you will use a lot in Project. This kind of command can either provide further alternatives or take immediate action. The Gantt Chart button, which is explained here, is a nice example:

- When the image portion of this command is clicked, the previously visible Gantt chart view is instantly displayed.
- You can view the available settings for this command by clicking on the text label portion of it (or simply the arrow, for commands with an arrow but no text label).

One instance of a split button is the Gantt Chart command. You should have no issue navigating the Project user interface if you are accustomed to using Office applications like Microsoft Word and Excel.

USE THE BACKSTAGE VIEW TO MANAGE FILES AND CONFIGURE SETTINGS

In addition to the standard file management actions (Open, New, Print, and Save), the Backstage view offers customization and sharing options that apply to the entire project.

The pages of the Backstage view are listed here in brief. Details about the active plan, including its start and end dates, statistics, and advanced properties, are also shown on the Info page. You collaborate with advanced attributes in "Start a new plan". You can also manage Project Web App accounts here if you're using Project Professional with the

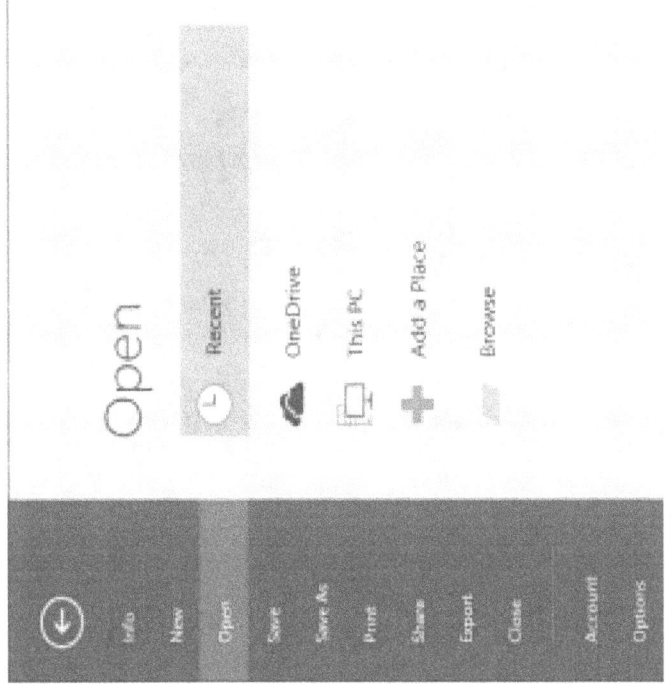

Project Web App. Options to create a new plan from scratch

or using a template are shown on the **New** page. Standard file-management commands include **Open**, **Save**, **Save As**, and **Close**. In addition to the print preview, the Print page offers alternatives for printing a plan. Options for attaching a plan to an email message and synchronizing with Microsoft SharePoint are available on the Share page. Along with other content exporting choices, the Export page offers the ability to create a copy of the plan in either PDF or XML Paper Specification (XPS) format. Connected services and Project details, including version information, are shown on the **Account** page. You may access services like roaming personal settings and Microsoft OneDrive file storage with a Microsoft account. The Project window's upper-right corner displays your user information while you are logged in.

The Project Options dialog box appears when you click **Options**. You can modify a variety of Project default settings and behaviors using the multiple pages in this dialog box, including whether you want to display the Start screen when Project launches.

Here are some pointers regarding settings and files:

- You can open a new blank plan by pressing the Esc key when you first launch Project and are at the Backstage view's New page.
- Recently opened plans can be pinned to the Open page's Recent Projects list.
- Click Pin To List from the shortcut menu that displays when you right-click on a plan name.
- By selecting the template and hitting the pin that shows up in the lower-right corner of the template preview, you can add your favorite templates to the New page.
- You will only see templates from your local computer if you are working offline.
- Click the Back button in the top-left corner of any Backstage page to close the Backstage view. The Esc key is another option.

CHAPTER TWO
TEMPLATES

You don't have to start from scratch. You may be able to utilize a template that contains a lot of the basic information you require, such as task names and relationships, rather than starting from scratch when making a plan. Templates can be found at: Project-installed templates.

Depending on the installation choices chosen when Project was set up on your machine, these may differ. Internet-based templates Microsoft offers a vast array of Project templates for free online download.

TEMPLATES IN YOUR COMPANY

It's possible that your company has a central template library. These templates frequently include specific task descriptions, resource allocations, and other organizationally specific information.

- Click the File tab, then select New to view the available templates.
- Templates show up on the Project Start screen.

Using the Import Wizard, Project can create a new file based on an existing file from Project or another program. You may turn your plans into templates that you can share or use later. The possibility that sharing plans include private data, such as resource pay rates, is a frequent worry. In addition to scheduling progress, you can choose to remove such information when creating a template from a plan. There is no change to the original plan.

HOW TO START A NEW PROJECT WITH A BLANK PLAN

- To access the Backstage view, select the File tab.
- To view the New page, click New.
- Select Blank Project.

HOW TO DEVELOP A NEW PLAN USING DATA IN A DIFFERENT FILE FORMAT, ANOTHER PLAN, OR A TEMPLATE

- Click New in the Backstage view.

Take any of these actions:

- To build a new plan (project) based on an existing one, click New From Existing Project.
- To build a new plan based on an Excel list, choose New From Excel Workbook.
- To build a new plan based on a SharePoint list, choose New From SharePoint Tasks List.

- To create a new project based on the template you prefer, click on it.

TO START A PROJECT

- Click Open in the Backstage view. Along with a list of previously opened plans, Project shows alternatives for opening plans.
- Decide on the site and opening strategy.

TO SAVE A PROJECT

- Select Save As in the Backstage view.
- Decide which folder and location to save the plan in.
- Click Save after entering a file name in the Save As dialog box.

USING AN EXISTING PLAN AS A TEMPLATE

- Click Export in the Backstage view.
- Select the Save Project As File option.
- Select Project Template under Save Project As File.
- Select "Save As."
- Select the folder in which the new template is to be created.
- Click Save after entering the desired template file name in the File Name box.

- Choose the kinds of data, including resource pay rates, that you wish to have deleted from the template when the Save As Template dialog box appears.
- Select "Save."

Work with the scheduling details displayed. You generate and manipulate the data in Views for your plan. The project incorporates a variety of viewpoints. Tables with graphics, tables with timeframes, tables by themselves, charts and diagrams, and forms are a few examples of perspectives. Certain views let you to define the kinds of data that are shown as well as filter, sort, or group data. In addition to building your own views, you can utilize and modify the views that are included with Project.

Many views are included in a project, although most people only work with one view at a time (or perhaps two in a split view, also called a combination view). Views are used for entering, editing, analyzing, and displaying project data. The Gantt With Timeline view is the default view that appears when you create a new plan. Views typically concentrate on the specifics of a task, resource, or assignment. For instance, in the Gantt Chart view, each task is graphically represented as a bar on the chart on the right side of the view, while task details are listed in a table on the left side of the view.

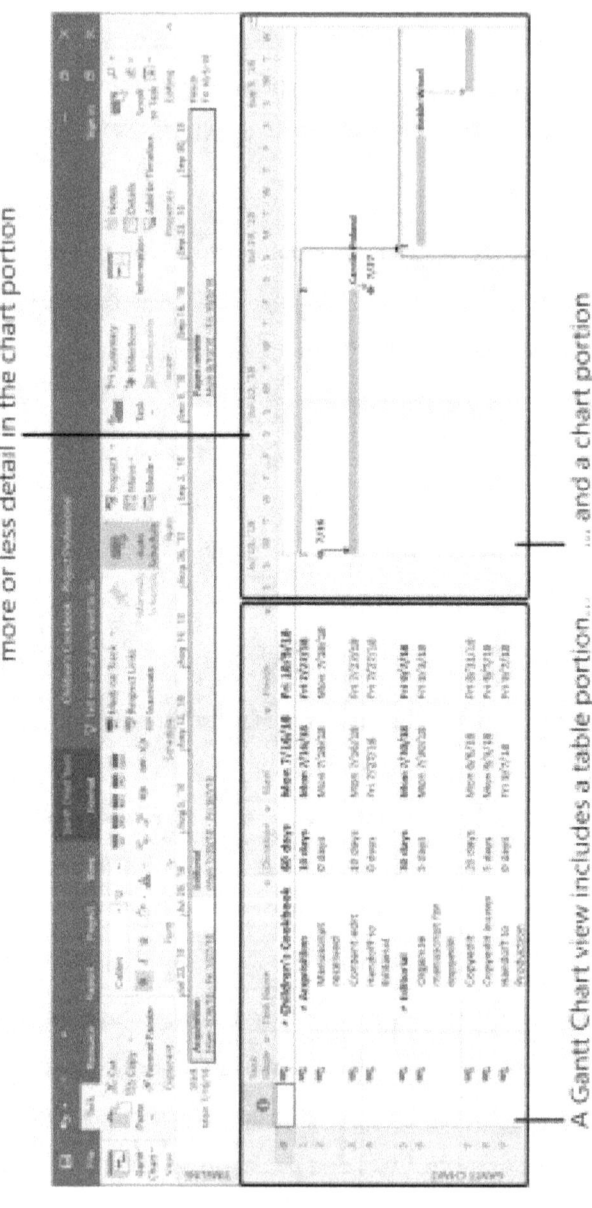

In Project, there are numerous additional perspectives. Remember that you are viewing distinct facets of the same set of plan data in each of the Project views. There may be too much information in even a basic plan to show all at once. To help you concentrate on the precise details you desire, use views.

HOW TO CHANGE BETWEEN VIEWPOINTS

Select the Task Views or Resource Views group on the View tab and take one of the following actions:

- Click the button for the desired view if it is displayed.
- Click Other Views, then select the desired view if the button for it is not visible.
- Click More Views, select the desired view, and then click Apply if it isn't in the Other Views menu.

HOW TO MODIFY A VIEW'S TIMESCALE

This action modifies the timeline in views that have one, such the Gantt chart. It modifies the amount of detail shown in other views.

- Take one of the actions listed below:
- Click the Zoom command in the Zoom group on the View tab, and then select the desired zoom level.

- Click Zoom Out or Zoom In on the Zoom Slider bar located in the status bar's lower-right corner.

To navigate to a different table in a view Only views with tables (like the Gantt chart) are affected by this action; views without tables (like the Calendar view) are not.

- Select Tables under the Data group on the View tab.
- Take one of the following actions: • Click the desired table if it is listed.
- Click More Tables, choose the desired table, and then click Apply if it isn't already listed.

HOW TO SHOW A SPLIT VIEW (COMBINATION)

- Select Details from the Split View group on the View tab.
- Select the view you wish to load into the split view's bottom pane by clicking on it in the Details box.

HOW TO MAKE THE TIMELINE VIEW VISIBLE OR INVISIBLE

- Select or clear the Timeline check box in the Split View group on the View tab.

UTILIZE REPORTS TO ASSESS THE PROGRESS OF A PROJECT

Reports can be used to present the data in your strategy in an engaging way. Charts, tables, and pictures are examples of items that can be used in reports to convey the progress of your plan. Task and resource statistics from your plan are displayed in reports. Reports can be printed like any other view or seen immediately in the Project window. Additionally, reports can be copied and pasted into other applications, such Microsoft PowerPoint. The project comes with a number of pre-made reports that you may use or modify, and you can even make your own.

Make a new plan and decide when it will begin. As one might anticipate, Project prioritizes timeliness. You may occasionally be aware of a project's anticipated start date, anticipated completion date, or both. But when working with Project, you simply specify one date—the start date or the finish date of the plan—rather than both. Why? Because Project determines the other date for you once you enter the start or finish date of the plan and other information. Keep in mind that Project is an active scheduling engine, not just a static store of your schedule data or a tool for creating Gantt charts. Even if you know that the plan should be completed by a specific date, most plans should be planned from a start date. Scheduling from a start date allows you the most scheduling flexibility and ensures that all tasks start as soon as possible. This flexibility

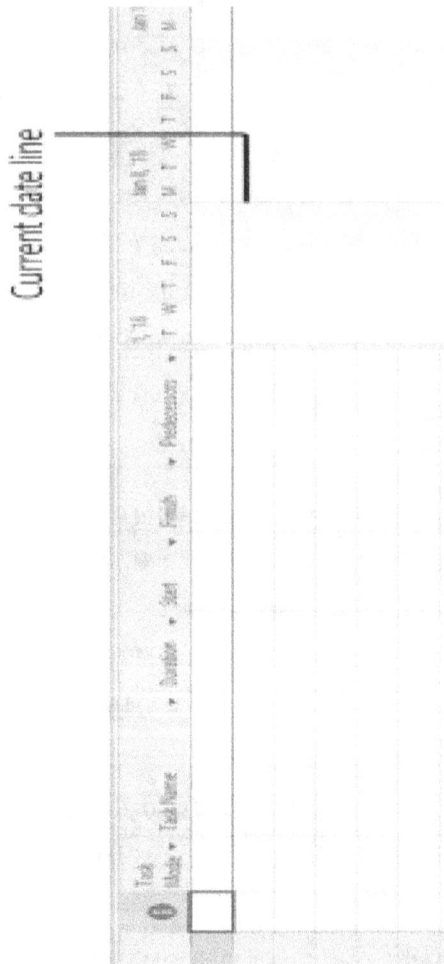

will be demonstrated in this and subsequent chapters when you work with a plan that is planned from a start date.

TO DEVELOP A FRESH STRATEGY

- Click the File tab in Project, if it's visible, and then select New.
- Select Blank Project or any other template from the list of available templates.

Or

- Select Blank Project or any other template from the list of possible templates that appears on the Start screen.

The start date of a new plan is set to the current day by Project. In the chart section of the Gantt Chart view, Project draws a thin green vertical line at the present day.

TO DETERMINE (OR MODIFY) THE COMMENCEMENT DATE OF THE PLAN

- Select Project Information from the Properties group on the Project tab.
- Enter the desired start date in the Start Date field of the Project Information dialog box, or choose one from the calendar by clicking the arrow.

ADVICE

To rapidly select the current day, click Today. Alternatively, you may use the calendar's left and right arrows to travel to any month and then click the desired date.

- To exit the Project Information dialog box and accept the start date, click OK.

HOW TO SAVE THE NEW PROJECT
- Select Save As after selecting the File tab.
- Select the place where you wish to save the plan on the Save As screen.

ADVICE

File-related Project settings are modifiable. For instance, you can configure Project to open the Project Information dialog box automatically whenever you make a new plan. Click Options after selecting the File tab to make this modification. Click Advanced in the Project Options dialog box, and then choose the Prompt For Project Info For New Projects check box in the General section. Additionally, you may set up Project to store the active plan automatically at specified intervals, such every ten minutes. Click Save in the Project Options dialog box, check the Auto Save Every box, and then choose the desired time period.

In the project calendar, indicate nonworking days.

The main tool for managing when each task and resource can be scheduled for work in a project is a calendar. We concentrate on the project calendar in this chapter, but you will work with additional calendar types in later chapters. The typical working and nonworking days and times for tasks are specified in the project calendar. Any one of the several base calendars that are included in a project might be used as the project calendar for a plan. In the Project Information dialog box, you choose the base calendar that will serve as the project calendar.

The three base calendars that come with Project are listed in the Calendar list:

- 24 Hours has no time off from work. Shift at Night covers a late-night "graveyard" shift pattern that runs from 11:00 p.m. to 8:00 a.m., Monday through Saturday, with a daily one-hour break.
- Typical Monday through Friday from 8:00 a.m. to 5:00 p.m., with a one-hour break every day, is the standard workday and week.
- The Standard calendar is the default, and only one of the base calendars can be used as the project calendar.

- Consider the project calendar to be the regular working days and hours of your company. For instance, this could be 8:00 a.m. to 5:00 p.m., Monday through Friday, with a one-hour lunch break in between. There may be deviations to this standard working schedule, such as holidays or vacation days, depending on your organization or particular resources.

The Change Working Time dialog box, which appears when you click the Change Working Time button on the Project tab, is where you modify calendars.

USE THE CHANGE WORKING TIME DIALOG BOX TO ALTER A CALENDAR'S WORKING HOURS

To establish regular working schedules and working time exceptions for certain resources or the entire plan, use this dialog box. Other typical instances of changes to working hours include: recurring vacations or other periods of time off that have a regular schedule, like weekly, monthly, or yearly.

Weekly variable working hours, for instance, to accommodate seasonal shifts in work schedules.

HOW TO CHOOSE THE PROJECT SCHEDULE

- Click the Project Information button in the Properties group on the Project tab.
- Select the calendar you wish to use as the project calendar by clicking the arrow in the Calendar box of the Project Information dialog box.

HOW TO DESIGNATE A PARTICULAR DATE AS NONWORKING

- Click the "Change Working Time" button in the Properties group on the Project tab.
- Provide a description of the exception in the Name field on the Exceptions tab in the bottom section of the Change Working Time dialog box.

Calendar exceptions do not have to be named, but it is a good idea for you or others to note the rationale for the exception.

- Type or choose the desired dates in the Start and Finish columns.
- Press OK.

HOW TO ESTABLISH A REGULAR NONWORKING PERIOD

- Click the "Change Working Time" button in the Properties group on the Project tab.

- Provide a description of the recurring exception in the Name field on the Exceptions tab of the Change Working Time dialog box.
- After selecting the Start field, select Details.
- Choose the desired recurrence values under Recurrence Patterns in the Details dialog box, and then click OK.
- To exit the Change Working Time dialog box, click OK.

HOW TO ARRANGE A SPECIAL WORK WEEK

- Click the "Change Working Time" button in the Properties group on the Project tab.
- In the bottom section of the Change Working Time dialog box, select the Work Weeks tab.
- Select a row beneath the value "[Default]".
- Type in a description and the range of dates that you would like the custom work week to be applicable.
- Choose or enter the range of dates that you would like the custom work week to apply for in the Start and Finish sections.
- Select Details.
- Choose the desired day and time values in the Details dialog box, then click OK.

- To exit the Change Working Time dialog box, click OK.

HOW TO ADD THE OTHER PROPERTIES AND THE PROJECT TITLE

Project monitors a number of document attributes, just like other Microsoft Office programs. Statistics like the number of revisions the document has undergone are among these attributes. Additional attributes encompass details that you may like to document regarding a plan, like the project title, the name of the project manager, or keywords to facilitate a file search. When printing, several of these attributes are utilized in page headers and footers, reports, and views. The Properties dialog box allows you to view and record these properties.

HOW TO ACCESS THE ATTRIBUTES OF A PLAN

- Select Info after selecting the File tab.
- Select Project Information from the Info screen's right side. Select the Advanced Properties option from the menu that displays.
- Click OK after entering the properties you wish to capture (all are optional).

Make a new plan and decide when it will begin. The scenario is that you will be a project manager at

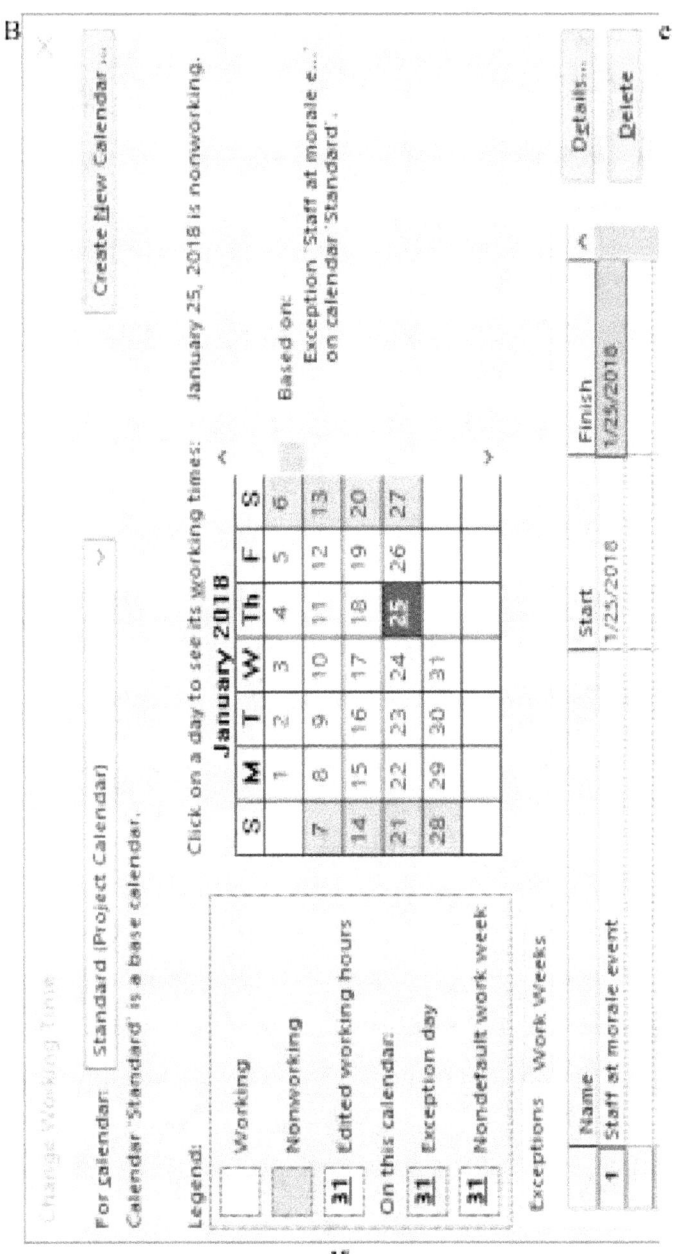

duration of this book. You have been requested to create a plan for the book launch of BookLove's upcoming big book.

Launch the project and complete these tasks:

- Using the Blank Project template as a guide, draft a new plan.
- Establish January 8, 2018 as the commencement date for the new plan.
- Save the modified strategy as Simple Plan.

In the project calendar, indicate nonworking days. The situation: You have to factor in a future date when all of the BookLove crew will be unavailable to work on the book launch project at BookLove Publishing. Proceeding with the Simple strategy, do the subsequent task:

Make a nonworking day calendar exemption for January 25, 2018, called Staff at an event, in the project calendar. Add the other properties and the plan title.

You wish to document high-level details regarding the new book launch strategy. These specifics pertain to crucial supplementary information you want to include in the plan but won't have an impact on the overall timetable. Proceeding with the Simple strategy, do the subsequent task: The most fundamental components of any project's plan are tasks. Tasks are the work that needs to be done in order to achieve the project's objectives. Tasks define the length, dependencies, and resource requirements of work. Project comprises a variety of responsibilities. These consist of milestones, subtasks, and summary tasks. In a broader sense, what are referred to as tasks in a project are occasionally referred to as activities or work packages.

Creating tasks, entering task durations and dates, creating milestone tasks, creating summary tasks, linking tasks to create dependencies, changing from manual to automatic task scheduling, verifying the duration and completion date of a plan, and documenting task information are all covered in this chapter.

MAKE TASKS

Tasks are the work that needs to be done in order to achieve the project's objectives. Although each task in a plan is assigned an ID number, the order in which tasks are completed is not always indicated by the number. There are two scheduling modes available for each work in Project: automatic scheduling and manual scheduling, which is the default. Consider a manually scheduled task as a starting point that you can modify at any moment without impacting the remaining tasks in the schedule. It's acceptable if you only know the task name to begin with. You can update the plan as you learn or determine new information regarding the task, such as when it should take place. Later in this chapter, in "Switch task scheduling from manual to automatic," you will work with automatic scheduling.

The first step in creating a task is, as you might expect, giving it a name. Because of this, it's worthwhile to establish sound procedures for naming tasks in your plans. Task names should be identifiable and make sense to the people who will do the tasks and to other stakeholders who will read the task names.

The following rules can help you come up with appropriate task names:

- Use succinct verb phrases, such "Edit manuscript," to convey the task at hand.
- Don't use information from the summary task name in the subtask name if the tasks will be arranged in an outline unless it clarifies the task.
- Don't include resource names in task names if resources will be assigned to the tasks.
- Don't worry about getting task names just perfect when you're first entering them into a plan; you can always change them later.

- Do your best to use clear, succinct language that conveys the necessary effort and makes sense to you and the people carrying out the task or going over the plan.
- You can also include more information in task notes, which are covered later in this chapter, if needed.

TO INPUT TASK NAMES

- In the Task Name column, click an empty cell.
- Type the names of your tasks here, followed by the Enter key.

TO ADD A NEW TASK TO A LIST OF TASKS

- Click in the column labeled "Task Name" to add the new task.
- Click Task in the Insert group on the Task tab. Project renumbers the tasks that follow and adds a row for a new task. The new task is named by the project.
- Type the task name while is selected, and then hit Enter.

TO REMOVE A TASK

- Click Delete Task after performing a right-click on the task name.

FOCUS OF PROJECT MANAGEMENT

Identifying the appropriate tasks for the delivery
Every project has a purpose or final objective, which is why it was initiated. This is referred to as the deliverable for the project. A physical object, like a new book, or a service or occasion, like a product launch party, could be this deliverable. A project manager must be able to define the appropriate tasks in order to produce the deliverable. All of the work necessary to successfully finish the project should be included in the task lists you make in Project. You may find it useful to differentiate between project and product scope when creating your task lists. The quality, attributes, and capabilities of the project's output are described by the product scope.

The duration of a task is the amount of time you anticipate needing to do it. Task lengths for a project might vary from minutes to months. You should probably deal with task durations on the scale of hours, days, and weeks, depending on the size of your plan. One advantage of utilizing a scheduling tool like Project over a to-do list or checklist is that you can assign duration values to your activities.

Microsoft Project Bible

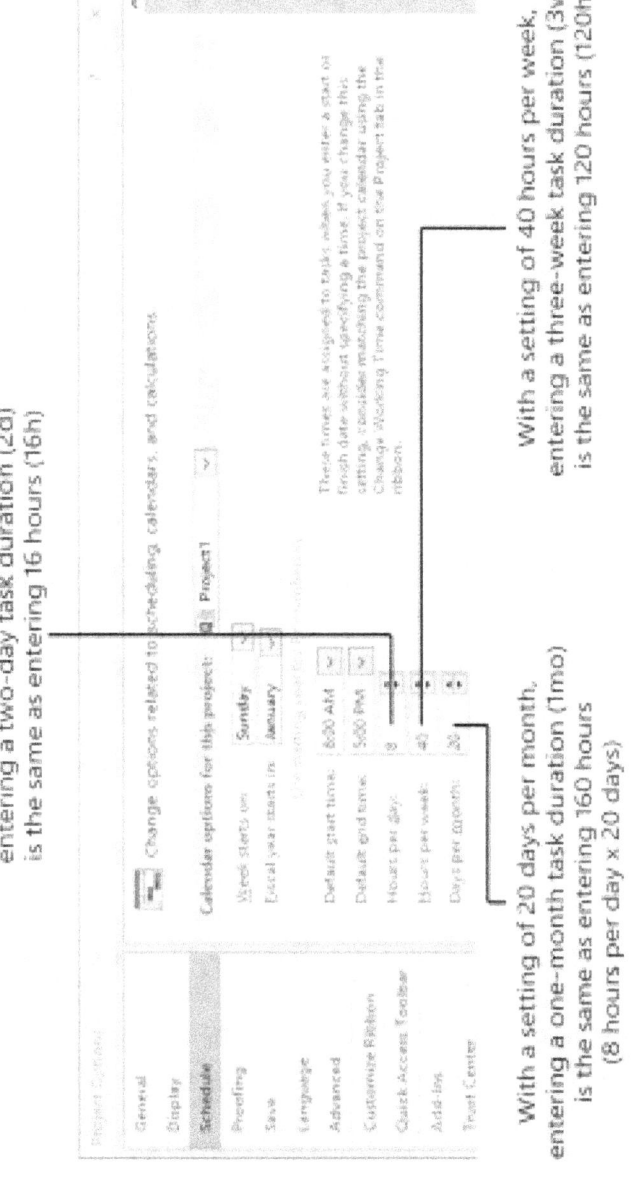

For durations, the project uses standard values for minutes and hours: One hour is equal to sixty minutes, and one minute is equivalent to sixty seconds.

You can utilize Project's default settings for days, weeks, and months (e.g., 20 days each month) or enter your own numbers in the Project Options dialog box. Control time-related parameters on the Project Options dialog box's Schedule tab. Using an example, let's examine task lengths. Consider a project calendar where the working hours are 8:00 a.m. to 5:00 p.m., Monday through Friday, with an hour off for lunch. The evenings (after 5:00 p.m.) and weekends are designated as nonworking hours. You may enter a task's duration as 2d to arrange work over two 8-hour workdays if you anticipate that it would take 16 hours of working time. Consequently, you should anticipate that if you begin the task at 8:00 a.m. on a Friday, it will not be finished until 5:00 p.m. on the Monday after. Due to the fact that Saturday and Sunday have been designated as nonworking days, no work would be scheduled during the weekend.

Project's default settings—eight hours per day, forty hours per week, and twenty days per month—are used for the practice assignments in this chapter. In fact, throughout this book we use Project's default settings unless specified otherwise.

- Click a cell in the task's Duration column to enter the task's duration.
- Type a value for the duration.

ADVICE

To enter or modify the value in the Duration field, you can also click the cell's up and down arrows.

All new tasks with a duration value are originally scheduled to begin on the project start date. This holds true regardless of whether the tasks are scheduled automatically or manually.

You can input a duration for manually scheduled tasks as either a numeric figure, like 2d, or as placeholder text, like Check with Marketing team. Point to the cell in any column that is too small to show the entire value; a ScreenTip will show the entire amount.

In the chart section of a Gantt chart view, Project displays a Gantt bar for tasks that are scheduled manually or automatically. The task's duration is indicated by the bar's length to plan a task with an elapsed duration that spans working and nonworking times 1. Use an e before the duration abbreviation when inputting the task's duration.

One full 24-hour day can be indicated by entering 1ed, seven 24-hour days by entering 1ew, or thirty 24-hour days by entering 1emo.

To determine how long a manually planned task will take 1. Enter or choose the desired start and finish dates in the task's Start and Finish fields. The duration value is calculated by the project. Keep in mind that the start and finish values may vary depending on predecessor relationships, the project start date, or other scheduling criteria after the task is turned to an automatically scheduled one. However, the duration value will remain unchanged. Put milestone tasks here. You could wish to include an important event in your project's plan, such the conclusion of a significant phase, in addition to activities that need to be finished. You will make a milestone task to do this. Milestones are important occasions that are either imposed upon the plan (like a grant application deadline) or reached inside it (like the conclusion of a work phase). Milestones are typically represented as tasks with 0 time because the milestone itself typically doesn't involve any effort. They use a diamond instead of a bar as their Gantt chart icon to graphically identify milestones. Any task, regardless of duration, can be marked as a milestone.

CHAPTER THREE

ENTERING A MILESTONE TASK

To enter a milestone task, do the following:

- Click the location where you wish to add the milestone in the Task Name column.
- Click Milestone in the Insert group on the Task tab.

The project renumbers future tasks and adds a new row for the new work. The project assigns a zero-day duration to the new task, which it names. Set a task's Duration value to 0 to turn it into a zero-duration milestone task.

HOW TO DESIGNATE A TASK AS A MILESTONE, REGARDLESS OF ITS DURATION

- Decide on a task title.
- Click Information in the Properties category on the Task tab.
- Select Advanced from the Task Information dialog box.
- Check the box to mark the task as a milestone.

Using summary tasks can help you arrange sets of closely connected tasks into an outline. In the plan's outline, a summary task consists of and provides an overview of the subtasks that are indented beneath it. The highest-level summary tasks are referred to as phases when they are arranged chronologically. An outline helps you and your stakeholders think in terms of major work items or phases while you are assessing a project's plan. For instance, book publishing projects are frequently separated into three stages: production, design, and editing. Once an outline has been made, it can be expanded or collapsed to provide the precise amount of detail you desire. Tasks are indented and outdented to produce an outline.

By default, summary tasks are scheduled automatically rather than by hand. Project measures the amount of time between the earliest start date and the latest completion date of its subtasks to determine how long an automatically scheduled summary task will take. An automatically scheduled summary task will change to a manually planned task if you make direct changes to its duration, start date, or finish time.

Similar to the duration of an automatically scheduled summary task, the duration of a manually scheduled summary task is determined by its subtasks. A manually scheduled summary task's duration can be changed, though, and Project will record both the estimated duration and the manual duration you set. The project summary task is the top level of a plan's overview. The project summary task is automatically generated by the project but is not displayed by default. Due to its position at the top of the plan's overview, the project summary task comprises rolled-up information from every task. It is a convenient way to view some important facts, such the plan's overall duration, as it also shows the entire duration of the plan.

- Choose the tasks you wish to summarize right below the assignment itself.
- Select the Indent Task button under the Schedule group on the Task tab.

To differentiate between summary tasks and subtasks, the project employs text and bar layout. When a manually planned, work is converted to a summary task, Project automatically schedules the new summary task.

HOW TO ADD A NEW SUMMARY TASK TO A LIST OF TASKS

- Decide which tasks will be subtasks and give them names.
- Select Summary from the Insert group on the Task tab.

The project renumbers the tasks that follow, inserts a row for the new task, and indents all of the selected tasks immediately below it. The new task is named <New Summary Task> by the project. Type the name of the summary task while <New Summary Task> is chosen. A summary task being downgraded to a task.

- Under the summary task, choose every subtask.
- Select the Outdent Task button under the Schedule group on the Task tab.

CONNECT TASKS TO ESTABLISH DEPENDENCIES

Tasks that are linked together establish scheduling links with one another. Because the beginning of one work depends on the completion of another, these task linkages are known as dependencies. Project can automatically modify the scheduling of linked activities when you construct task dependencies, also known as linkages, in response to modifications in your plan. To fully utilize the project scheduling engine, dependencies must be created by connecting tasks.

Any task can serve as a predecessor to one or more tasks that follow. Similarly, every task might be a follow-up to one or more activities that came before it.

A task may have distinct task links with each of its two or more successor tasks. For instance, one successor may have a finish-to-start relationship with the predecessor task, whereas another successor may have a finish-to-finish relationship.

Using a genuine scheduling tool, like Project, is very beneficial when handling changes to scheduled start and finish dates and representing task relationships. For instance, Project will reschedule tasks if you alter their durations or add or delete activities from a chain of connected tasks.

When the details of an automatically scheduled task change, it is dynamically rescheduled. You can make a manually planned task respect its predecessor links at any time, but manually scheduled tasks are not rescheduled by scheduling adjustments to their predecessor tasks. In essence, you may "nudge" a manually planned task to honor its connections.

Task associations can show up in Project in a number of forms, such as the following:

- Task relationships are shown as the lines that connect tasks in Gantt charts and Network Diagram views.
- Task ID numbers of predecessor tasks show up in the Predecessor fields of successor tasks in tables like the Entry table. (To see the Predecessor column in a

Gantt chart view, you may need to pull the vertical divider bar to the right.)

ADVICE

By including lead and lag timings, you can modify the relationship between predecessor and successor tasks in the schedule. You can, for instance, establish a two-day delay between the conclusion of one work and the beginning of its successor.

HOW TO CONNECT TASKS

- Decide which task names you wish to link. Holding down the Ctrl key while selecting the first task will allow you to select the additional work or tasks if they are not contiguous.
- Click the Link the Selected Tasks button (which resembles two chain links) in the Schedule group on the Task tab.

The project establishes a finish-to-start relationship between the tasks. Linking tasks together creates schedule dependencies between them.

- Drag down to the task bar for the successor task after pointing to the predecessor task bar in the chart section of a Gantt chart view.

It should be noted that when you drag, the pointer shifts to a pop-up window and link icon that updates with data as you point to other task bars. You can use this tooltip to link tasks with the mouse. When you are linking tasks, the pointer changes.

- Let go of the mouse button once the pointer crosses the successor task bar. Dragging the pointer from the Gantt bar of the predecessor to the Gantt bar of the successor is one method of linking tasks.

Or

- Enter the ID of the predecessor task in the successor task's Predecessors field. To see the Predecessor column, you may need to scroll the table to the right.

ADVICE

You have two options when working with summary tasks: **you can link the most recent task in the first phase with the earliest task in the second phase, or you can link summary tasks directly.** In either case, the scheduling outcome is the same. However, you are never allowed to attach a summary task to one of its own subtasks. Project forbids it since it leads to a circular scheduling issue.

Alternately, choose the task for which you wish to define one or more precursor tasks.

- Click the Information button in the Properties group on the Task pane.
- Click OK after selecting or entering the task name or ID value of the desired predecessor task on the Predecessors tab of the Task Information dialog box.

One useful method for providing several predecessors for a single successor task is to add predecessor tasks using the task Information dialog box.

HOW TO DISCONNECT TASKS

- Decide which tasks you wish to delink.
- Click the Unlink Tasks button (which resembles a broken chain link) in the Schedule group on the Task tab.

To make a manually scheduled task adhere to the scheduling outcome of its predecessor

- Based on the relationships between its predecessor tasks, choose the manually scheduled task that needs to be postponed.
- Select the Respect Links button under the Schedule category on the Task tab.

63

Change the manual task schedule to an automatic one.

By default, the project schedules new tasks manually. Actually, you have only worked with manually scheduled activities. You have two options for managing task scheduling in Project:

- To quickly capture some details, work with manually planned activities without scheduling them. Consider a manually scheduled task as a starting point that you can modify at any moment without impacting the remaining elements of the plan. It's acceptable if at first you only know the name of a task. You can update the plan as you learn or determine new information regarding the task, such as when it should take place.
- To fully utilize Project's robust scheduling system, work with automatically scheduled tasks.

HOW TO CHANGE THE MANUAL SCHEDULING OF SPECIFIC TASKS OR THE FULL PLAN TO AN AUTOMATED ONE

Project gives tasks that are automatically scheduled a duration as well as start and end dates. When a plan changes, automated scheduling allows a project to automatically update calculated schedule parameters, including task durations, start and finish dates, and more. Project may additionally recalculate impacted tasks in response to modifications to calendars and task linkages.

To change the scheduling of a single task from manual to automatic:

- Choose the manually planned task that you wish to modify.
- Click the chosen task's Task Mode field, and then click the arrow that shows up.
- Select Auto Scheduled from the list that displays.

Several tasks will be moved from manual to automatic task scheduling.

- Choose the manually planned tasks you wish to modify.
- Click the Auto Schedule button in the Tasks group on the Task pane.

HOW TO CONVERT THE EXISTING OPEN PLAN'S WORK SCHEDULING FROM MANUAL TO AUTOMATIC

- Click the Mode button in the Tasks group on the Task tab, and then select Auto Schedule.

Or

- Click the text in the New Tasks status bar.
- Select the preferred scheduling mode.

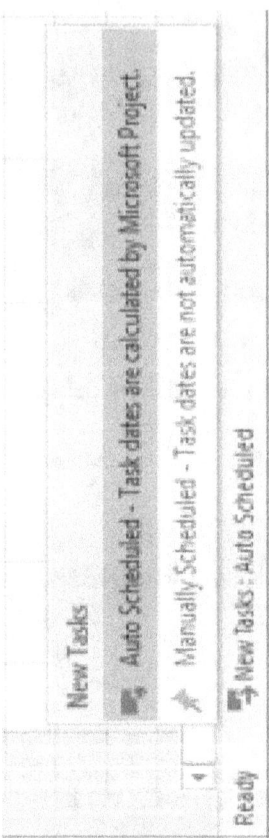

HOW TO MODIFY THE PROJECT'S DEFAULT SCHEDULING MODE FOR ALL NEW TASKS

- Click Options on the File tab, and then select the Schedule tab in the Project Options dialog box.

- Select All New Projects from the Scheduling Options For This Project box, and then select Auto Scheduled from the New Tasks Created box.
- Press OK.

Verify the duration and completion date of a plan. You and other project stakeholders will want to know how long a project is likely to take at any point during planning or execution. It is not necessary to enter the entire project duration or completion date in a plan. The task durations, dependencies, project calendar modifications, and several other elements you have noted in a plan are the basis on which Project determines these values. The project determines the plan's completion date by counting the number of working days needed to finish the tasks, beginning on the plan's start date. Project recalculates the completion date if the start date is altered. By counting the working days between the earliest start date and the latest completion date of the plan's tasks, the project calculates the plan's duration. The length of a task does not always correspond to the amount of time that has passed since Project makes a distinction between working and nonworking time.

The Timeline view, the project summary task, and the Project Statistics dialog box are some convenient ways to view the duration of the plan and the scheduled start and conclusion dates.

Project Statistics for 'Simple Tasks'				X
	Start		Finish	
Current	Mon 1/8/18		Tue 2/6/18	
Baseline	NA		NA	
Actual	NA		NA	
Variance	0d		0d	
	Duration	Work		Cost
Current	21d?	0h		$0.00
Baseline	0d	0h		$0.00
Actual	0d	0h		$0.00
Remaining	21d?	0h		$0.00
Percent complete: Duration: 0% Work: 0%				Close

CRUCIAL

Select the Timeline check box in the Split View group on the View tab if the Timeline view is not visible. In the Statistics dialog box, you may view a plan's duration, completion date, and other details.

- Click the Project Information button in the Properties group on the Project tab.
- Select Statistics from the Project Statistics dialog box.

HOW TO SHOW THE TASK FOR THE PROJECT SUMMARY

- In a Gantt chart view, click anywhere. The Format tab is labeled Gantt Chart Tools when the focus is on a Gantt chart view.
- Choose the Project Summary Task from the Show/Hide group on the Format tab checkbox.

At the top of the Gantt Chart view, Project shows the project summary task with ID 0.

You'll see a Gantt chart derived from the start and end dates of the overall plan, together with the same duration and start and finish figures shown in Project Statistics. Record the work details. In a note, you can include more details about a task. For instance, you may want to keep the task name brief yet provide thorough details about the assignment. Instead of including these facts in the task name, you can provide them in a task note. In this manner, the data is included inside the plan and is readily readable or printable. Task notes, resource notes, and assignment notes are the three different categories of notes. The Task Information dialog box's Notes tab allows you to enter and examine task notes. Numerous text formatting choices are supported by Project Notes, and you may also store or link to graphic pictures and other file kinds within notes.

Notes that are too lengthy to fit in a ScreenTip can be shown in full text by double-clicking the note icon. A task note is also supported by the previously described project summary task. The project summary task is a fantastic area to record critical details about the plan because it covers the complete plan. Text placed in the Properties dialog's Comments field box shows up on the project summary task as a note. Any changes you make to the project summary task will be reflected in the Properties dialog box's Comments area. Occasionally, you may wish to link a task in a plan to data that is kept on a webpage or in another document. You can use hyperlinks to link a particular assignment, resource, or task to more information that is located outside of the plan.

HOW TO INCLUDE A MESSAGE IN A TASK

- Choose the task name that you wish to include a message on.
- Click the Notes button in the Properties group on the Task pane.

Alternately, right-click the task name and select Notes.

- Type the desired note text in the Notes box, then select OK.

HOW TO GIVE A TASK A HYPERLINK

- To open the Insert Hyperlink dialog box, right-click the task name and select Hyperlink.
- Type the link text you wish to show in the Text to display box.
- Type the URL of the destination address you wish to link to in the Address box.
- Press OK.

ADVICE

Either click the hyperlink icon or right-click it, select Hyperlink from the shortcut menu that displays, and then select Open Hyperlink to launch the webpage in your browser. To swiftly eliminate formatting, notes, or hyperlinks from certain tasks, **Click the Clear button**

Jason Taylor

(which resembles an eraser) in the Editing group on the Task tab, and then choose the desired command.

CHAPTER FOUR
MAKE TASKS

The situation: You work for BookLove Publishing as a project manager. You are prepared to begin after gathering the basic task names for the launch of a new book. Launch Project and carry out the following actions in the SimpleBuildTaskList plan:

- Type in the task names shown below: Assign people to the launch team; create and order marketing collateral; distribute advance copies; organize magazine feature stories; and open a public book portal. You discover you missed a task while going over the ones you entered. Next, you'll add that task.
- To make it appear above the Distribute advance copies task, add a new task called Public Launch Phase.
- Enter the dates and durations of the tasks.

The situation: You presented your initial task list to the other project stakeholders as well as the resources who would carry out the work. You would like to include their first (although insufficient) input on certain assignment durations and dates in the revised book launch plan.

●	Task Mode	Task Name	Duration	Start	Finish	Predecessors	Jan 7, '18 T F S S M
1	⚘	Assign launch team members					
2	⚘	Design and order marketing material					
3	⚘	Public Launch Phase					
4	⚘	Distribute advance copies					
5	⚘	Coordinate magazine feature articles					
6	⚘	Launch public web portal for book					

Proceed with the following tasks in the SimpleBuildTaskList plan:

- Give task 1 a one-day length and assign launch team members.
- For the remaining challenges, type the following text phrases or durations.
- Enter 1/22/18 in the Start field and 1/30/18 in the Finish field. Coordinate magazine feature articles.

According to the project, it will take six days. The first week's Monday through Wednesday and Friday, followed by Monday and Tuesday of the following week, constitutes six working days. The Gantt chart for the assignment is additionally drawn by the project to include the nonworking days (the Thursday, January 25 morale event you set up in "Start a new plan") as well as the weekend in between these working days.

- Open a public booking portal. You don't yet know the start or end date or duration, but you can still record what you do know.
- Type "approximately two weeks before launch complete" in the Start column.

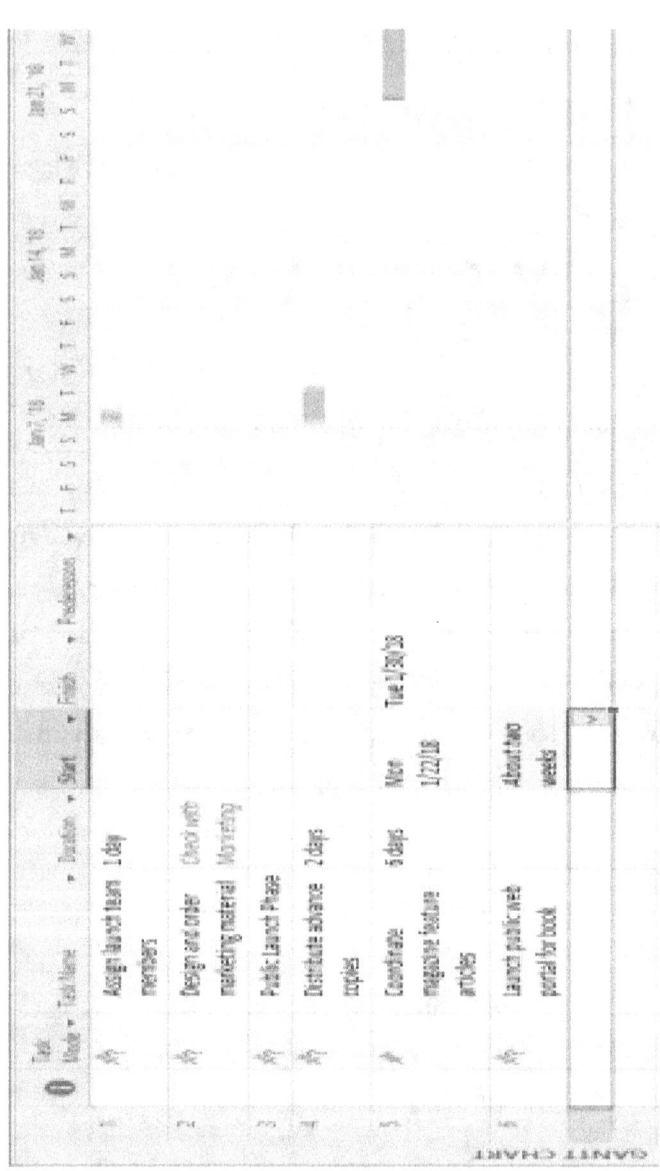

Put milestone tasks here.

The situation: You recently found out when the planning tasks for the new book launch must be finished in order for it to happen on schedule. In the plan, you want this date to be visible. Proceed with the following task in the SimpleBuildTaskList plan:

- To make it appear above Public Launch Phase, add a new milestone task called Planning complete.

	Task Mode	Task Name	Duration	Start	Finish	Predecessors	Jan 7, '18 T F S S M T
1	⭐	Assign launch team members	1 day				
2	⭐	Design and order marketing material	*Check with Marketing*				
3	⭐	Planning complete	0 days				1/8
4	⭐	Public Launch Phase					

Make a list of summary tasks to provide a plan overview.

The situation: The plan for launching the new book has been sufficiently developed to be divided into two stages.

	Task Mode	Task Name	Duration	Start	Finish	Predecessors
1		▲ Planning Phase	1 day	Mon 1/8/18	Mon 1/8/18	
2	☆	Assign launch team members	1 day			
3	☆	Design and order marketing		Check with Marketing		
4	☆	Planning complete	0 days			1/8
5		▲ Public Launch Phase	6 days	Mon 1/22/18	Tue 1/30/18	
6	☆	Distribute advance copies	2 days			
7	☆	Coordinate magazine feature articles	6 days	Mon 1/22/18	Tue 1/30/18	
8	☆	Launch public web portal for		About two weeks		

Proceed with the following tasks in the SimpleBuildTaskList plan:

- Assign the Public Launch Phase task as the task summary.
- Distribute advance copies through.
- Open the book's public website.
- Take note of how establishing the summary task affects scheduling. Project fixed the start date of the summary task (as well as its other duration-based subtask) to January 22 because task 6 already had established start and finish dates.
- Include tasks 1 through 3 in a new summary task called Planning Phase, making them its subtasks.

Connect tasks to establish dependencies. The situation: Everything is going well with the new book launch plan. You are now prepared to establish task linkages after the tasks have been delineated under summary tasks.

Proceed with the following tasks in the SimpleBuildTaskList plan:

- To establish a finish-to-start relationship between tasks 2 and 3, enter a task ID in the Predecessor field. Keep in mind that task 3 had no start or ending date before, but by designating it as task 2's successor, you provided Project with sufficient details to assign a start date: January 9th, the working day after task 2's completion.

- Next, you'll use a different method to connect tasks three and four.
- Use the Task Information dialog box to create task 3, Design and order marketing material, which is the forerunner of task 4.
- Use the Link the Selected Tasks command to link all subtasks under the Public Launch Phase (tasks 6 through 8) simultaneously.

Pay attention to task 8's text value in the Start field, which reads "About two weeks." As you can see, Project provided the normal one-day length and substituted a planned date for the text value in task 8's Start field. The project took this action as, as soon as the task was connected to another activity, it needed a date value. The duration value is followed by a question mark, which signifies that it is an estimate and has no bearing on the task's scheduling.

- Use your mouse to navigate from task 1, Planning Phase, to task 5, Public Launch Phase, in the Gantt Chart view's chart section.

- Task 3's length should be changed from the placeholder phrase Check with Marketing to two weeks, as the BookLove marketing team has reported that this is the approximate time frame.
- You'll see that the Planning Phase summary task's new length resulted in duration to rise, however the task 4 milestone's scheduling remained unaffected. Why not? Keep in mind that this activity is still planned by hand. In the following step, you will compel Project to modify the start and end dates of this task in order to respect the start and finish dates of its predecessor work, leaving it as manually scheduled.
- Modify task 4, Planning Complete, to honor the previous connection.

Task 4 is rescheduled by the project to begin when task 3 is finished.

The Public Launch Phase summary task's beginning disregards its connection to its predecessor, the Planning Phase summary task, as you may have observed. Unlike task 4, the Public Launch Phase summary task will not be rescheduled when the Respect Link button is clicked while it is chosen. This is due to the fact that the earliest start and latest finish dates of the summary task's subtasks—which in

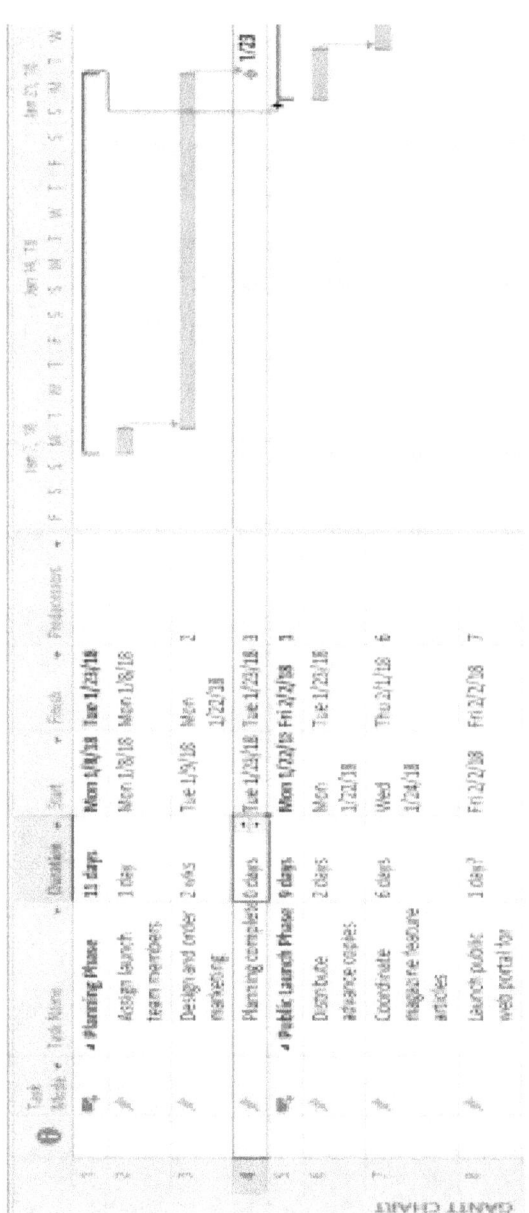

this instance are still manually scheduled—determine the

start and finish dates of the summary task. Change the manual task schedule to an automatic one. The scenario: Other project stakeholders and the resources that will do the work have examined the updated book launch plan. You have enough faith in the strategy as a whole to go from manual to automatic task scheduling, even if you anticipate some changes as you gain more knowledge about the book launch.

Proceed with the following tasks in the SimpleBuildTaskList plan:

- Using the Auto Schedule command on the Task tab, set tasks two through four to be scheduled automatically. To show that the tasks are now automatically scheduled, Project modifies the Task Mode icons and the Gantt bar formatting.
- To set task 6 to be automatically scheduled, use the task Mode box. Task 6 was postponed to begin later this time. What caused this to occur? Remember that the two summary tasks are dependent on each other. The dependence essentially said that the Public Launch Phase should begin upon completion of the Planning Phase. However, the project did not rearrange the subtasks to take this dependency into consideration because task 6 and the other Public

Launch Phase subtasks were manually planned. The project also changed the start date as soon as you put task 6 on automatic scheduling of its synopsis. Project did not reschedule the remaining subtasks 7 and 8, which are still manually scheduled.

- Use your preferred technique to schedule tasks 7 and 8 automatically. The remaining tasks are rescheduled by the project. As a result, the Public Launch Phase and the project's overall timeframe are prolonged. This plan is currently configured to handle any additional tasks you input as manually scheduled. You might leave this setting alone and then set up automated scheduling for certain tasks. But now that this strategy is sufficiently established, automatic scheduling can be used. Later on, if necessary, you can manually schedule certain specified tasks.
- Modify the plan to automatically schedule all upcoming tasks.
- Enter a new task named Launch social media programs for book below task 8. The new task is added to the plan by the project. By default, it has a one-day duration, is scheduled to begin on the start date of its summary task, and is not connected to any other tasks.

Jason Taylor

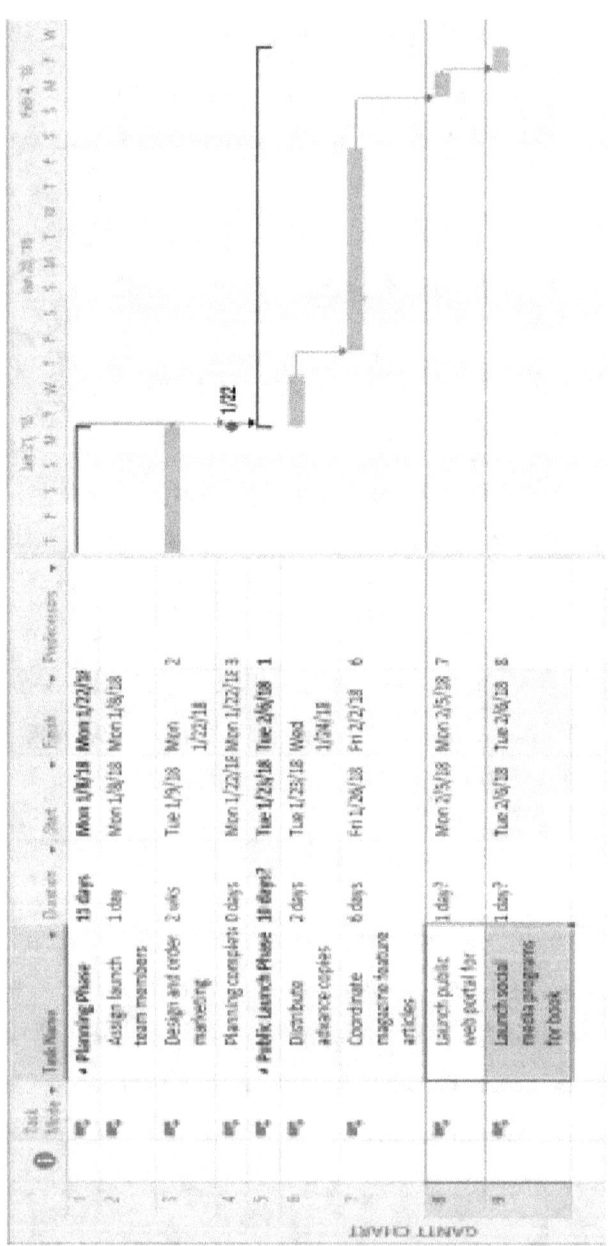

Microsoft Project Bible

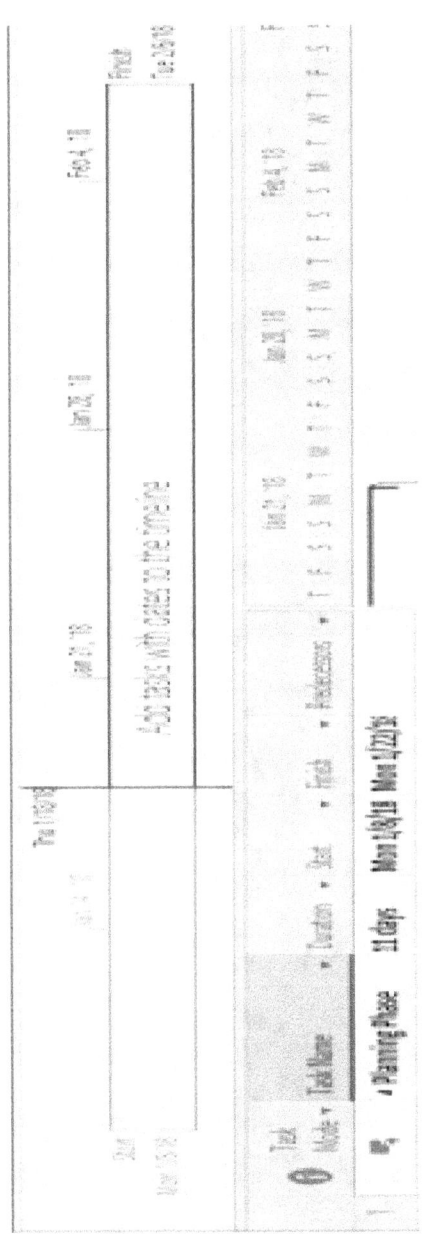

The two tasks are linked by the project. You'll see that the Public Launch Phase summary task's duration was automatically changed from nine to ten days.

Verify the duration and completion date of a plan. The situation: The team is more prepared for the forthcoming work thanks to your preparation for the new book launch. The current duration and completion date of the book launch are often requested from you. Proceed with the following tasks in the SimpleBuildTaskList plan:

- Take note of the plan's current start and end dates in the Timeline view.
- In the Project Information dialog box, locate the plan's completion date.
- Next, examine the Project Statistics dialog box's duration data in further detail.
- Show the task summary for the project on the Gantt chart view.

Record the work details.

You would like to include some information on a few tasks in the new book launch plan. Keeping such facts in the plan will benefit you later on, and it will also be helpful to other project stakeholders who may use the plan in the future. Proceed with the following tasks in the SimpleBuildTaskList plan:

- Include the note Obtain the publicist's list of recipients for task 6 and distribute advance copies.

- Point to task 6's note icon. A ScreenTip displays the note. For task 0, the project summary task, you may see a note icon. Next, we'll examine that.
- Point to task 0's note icon. The note that appears in the ScreenTip.
- Include the text of the hyperlink. Include the company's address in the spring catalog here.

Open the public book portal.

The indicators column has a hyperlink icon. The descriptive text you previously supplied is displayed when you point to the icon. When it comes to resource management and cost monitoring, projects can assist you in making better judgments.

HOW TO INPUT THE NAMES OF WORK RESOURCES

- To open the Resource Sheet view, select Resource Sheet within the Resource Views group on the View tab.
- In the Resource Name column, click an empty cell.
- Type the names of your resources, hitting Enter after each one. In the Type field, Project uses the Work resource type by default.

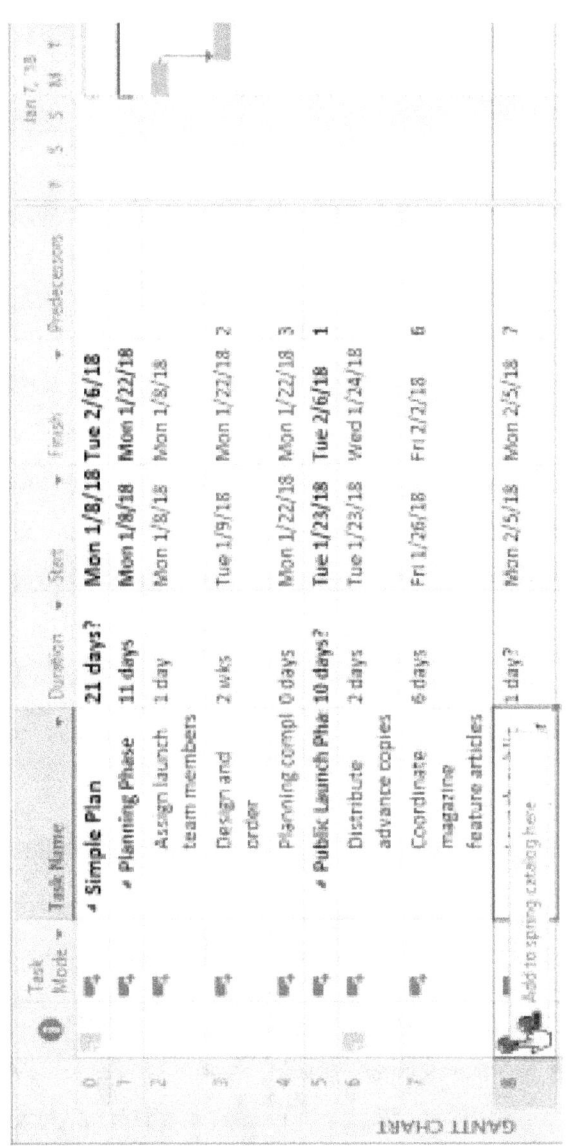

ADVICE

Resources from your email address book are easily importable. Change to the Resource Sheet view first. Next, select Add Resources from the Resource menu.

To add a new work resource to a list of resources.

- Show the view of the Resource Sheet.
- To add the new resource, click in the cell in the Resource Name column.
- Click Add Resources in the Insert group on the Resource tab, followed by Work Resource. The project renumbers the resources that follow and adds a new row with the name in the Resource Name column.
- Type the resource name while is chosen, and then hit Enter.

HOW TO REMOVE A RESOURCE

- Click Delete Resource after performing a right-click on the resource name.
- Enter the work resources' maximum capacity.

Project management assists you in managing the restricted capacity of work resources inside a plan. A resource's maximum ability to do the tasks given to it is indicated by the Max. Units parameter. When a resource's maximum units are 100%, it indicates that all of its working time is accessible to complete the tasks specified in the plan. If you give a resource to more tasks than it can complete, Project will notify you with an indicator and formatting. When a resource is dedicated to two or more tasks at 100% capacity each and the tasks overlap, for instance, it is said to be overallocated. For new work resources, the default Max. Units value is 100%.

You can specify a bigger maximum units value to indicate the number of available people for a resource that reflects a category of interchangeable individuals with a common skill set rather than a specific individual. For instance, entering 200% as the maximum unit value

Using such a resource implies that you anticipate having two individuals who fall into that resource category available to work full-time each day, or four individuals available to work half-time each day, or any comparable combination. You can enter a lower maximum unit's value for a resource that is not available full-time. You can expect that resource's capacity to be three-quarters of a full-time resource, for instance, by setting a maximum unit's value of 75%. This equates to 30 hours of capacity for a 40-hour work week. It should be noted that a full-time employee assigned to a certain project only part-time or a part-time employee may be subject to such a part-time working capacity.

To modify the working capability of a resource

- Select Resource Sheet from the Resource Views group on the View tab.
- Select the Max. Units field for the resource you wish to modify in the Resource Sheet view (the Max. component of the field's column heading may be the only part displayed).

ADVICE

- Up and down arrows show up when you click on a numeric number in a field such as Max. Units.
- You have the option of entering the desired number directly in the field or clicking these to show it.
- Type the resource's updated value. To indicate two resources, for instance, put 200%; to indicate a resource with only half-time availability, enter 50%.
- Instead of displaying and entering maximum units as percentages (like 50%, 100%, or 400%), you can choose to display and enter them as partial or whole numbers (like 0.5, 1, or 4).

- Click Options on the File tab to use this format. Click the Schedule tab in the Project Options dialog box. Click Decimal in the Show Assignment Units As A box under the Schedule title.
- Enter the pay rates for work resources. Cost restricts the scope of many initiatives, and almost all projects have some financial component.

The project manager can respond to crucial queries like:

- What is the anticipated overall cost of the project based on task durations and resource assignments? by monitoring and controlling cost information in the project.
- Is the company spending a lot of money on work that might be done with less expensive resources? How much will a certain kind of work or resource cost during the course of the project? Is the company spending money at a pace that it can maintain for the project's anticipated duration?

In addition to overtime rates for work resources, you may specify regular rates and prices per usage for both labor and material resources in Project. Keep in mind that there are three different kinds of resources in a project: material, cost, and labor.

There are several time bases with which you can enter pay rates: per minute, hourly (by default), daily, weekly, monthly, or annually. Rates are entered using the rate/period format, such as 30/h for $30 per hour. Minutes are abbreviated as /m, hours as /h, days as /d, weeks as /w, months as /mo, and years as /y.

Project determines the assignment's cost after a work resource is assigned to a task and has a standard pay rate entered. Project accomplishes this by multiplying the resource's pay rate by the allocated work value, both using a similar time increment (e.g., hours). The expenses per resource, task, and assignment are then displayed to you (as well as the prices rolled up to summary tasks and the full plan).

Overtime charges are handled differently by each project. Only when you explicitly enter overtime hours for an assignment does the project apply the overtime pay rate. Because there is too much of a potential that it will apply overtime when you did not intend it to, the project does not automatically calculate overtime hours and related costs.

You can configure Project to automatically apply standard or overtime pay rates whenever you add a new resource if you work with a lot of resources that have the same pay rates.

Click Options on the File tab to accomplish this. Click Advanced in the Project Options dialog box. Enter your preferred default pay rates under the General Options For This Project section. When work resource standards and overtime expenses should be incurred is up to you to decide. The choices are made at the beginning of a task, at the conclusion of the activity, or prorated (the default) equally over the task's duration.

A resource may include a fixed price that Project applies to each task to which the resource is assigned, either in place of or in addition to cost rates. We refer to this as a cost per use. The cost per use is not affected by the length of the task or the quantity of work the resource completes on it, in contrast to cost rates. Use the Resource Sheet view to see a resource's pay rates and other cost-related information.

HOW TO INPUT A RESOURCE'S STANDARD RATE

- Select Resource Sheet from the Resource Views group on the View tab.
- To establish a standard pay rate for a resource, select the Std. Rate box in the Resource Sheet view. Only Std. may appear in the column heading, depending on the column's width.

- Use the rate/period format to enter a conventional rate, such 30/h.

HOW TO INPUT A RESOURCE'S OVERTIME RATE

- Show the view of the Resource Sheet.
- To establish an overtime, pay rate for a resource, click the Ovt. Rate column. You may only see Ovt. in the column title, depending on how wide the column is.
- Use the rate/period format to enter an overtime rate, such as 45/h.

HOW TO INPUT A RESOURCE'S COST PER USE

- Show the view of the Resource Sheet.
- Type the desired figure in the Cost/Use field.

Work schedule adjustments in a resource calendar Different calendar types are used by projects for various objectives. Resource calendars are the main topic of discussion here. The working and nonworking hours of a particular resource are managed by a resource calendar. To decide when work on a resource can be planned, the project makes use of a resource calendar. Resource calendars do not apply to material or cost resources; they only apply to work resources (people and equipment).

Project generates a resource calendar for every work resource when you first create them in a plan. The project calendar, which is the Standard base calendar by default, has the exact same beginning working-time settings as resource calendars. With one hour off for lunch every day, the Standard base calendar, which is integrated into Project, supports a default work schedule of 8:00 AM to 5:00 PM, Monday through Friday.

You don't need to change any resource calendars if all of your resources' working hours coincide with the project calendar's working hours. But it's likely that certain of your resources will require exceptions to the project calendar's working hours, like: a flexible employment arrangement. Other periods, like training or conference attendance, when a resource is unavailable to work on the project.

ADVICE

You might be tempted to arrange the resource's working hours in your project to correspond with a part-time schedule, such 8:00 A.M. to 12:00 P.M. every day, if they are available to work on it just part-time. A preferable strategy, though, would be to appropriately modify the resource's availability, as shown in the Max. Units field—in this case, to 50%. Modifying the resource's unit availability maintains the focus on the resource's ability to complete the project, not on the precise times of day when that work may be completed. In the Resource Sheet view, you can specify a resource's maximum units. Resource calendars created from the same project calendar immediately update when you make changes to the project calendar. However, keep in mind that once you create a resource calendar exception, it will not be impacted by further modifications to the project calendar that occur during the same time frame.

Assigning a new base calendar to a resource or group of resources may be simpler if you find that you need to make comparable changes to multiple resource calendars (for example, to manage a night shift). Compared to changing individual resource calendars, this is more efficient, and if necessary, you can use the base calendar to make changes across the entire plan. For instance, you can use the Night Shift base calendar for resources who work the night shift if your project involves both day and night shifts. The Change Working Time dialog box allows you to modify a base calendar. In the Resource Sheet view, you may choose a particular base calendar for resource collections right from the Base Calendar column on the Entry table.

CHAPTER FIVE
WORK RESOURCE

To give a work resource a calendar exception

- Select Change Working Time from the Properties group on the Project tab.
- Click the name of the resource whose calendar you wish to modify in the For calendar box.

Keep a close eye on the value in the For Calendar field when working in the Change Working Time dialog box. Editing the incorrect calendar by accident is not difficult.

- Provide a description of the exception in the Name field on the Exceptions tab in the dialog box's lower section. For you and anybody else who might examine the plan later, the calendar exception description serves as a helpful reminder. Type or choose the desired dates in the Start and Finish columns.
- Click Details to create a partial working-time exception for a resource, such as a section of a day when the resource is unavailable. You can also make recurrent exceptions to the resource's availability in the Details dialog box.

The Change Working Time dialog box allows you to review or create working time calendar exceptions for specific resources.

- To exit the Change Working Time dialog box, click OK.

HOW TO CHANGE THE DEFAULT WORKING WEEK DAYS AND TIMINGS FOR A RESOURCE

- The Change Working Time dialog box will appear.
- Click the name of the resource whose calendar you wish to modify in the For calendar box.
- Select the tab for Work Weeks.
- Click Details after selecting [Default] right beneath the Name column heading.
- Choose the day or days you wish to change under Selected Day(s).

Take any of these actions:

- Click Set days to nonworking times to make all days nonworking.
- Click establish day(s) to these if you want to establish working hours that are different from the default calendar certain working hours, and then enter the working hours in the From and To columns.

- Click Use times from base calendar for these days to go back to the base calendar working hours.

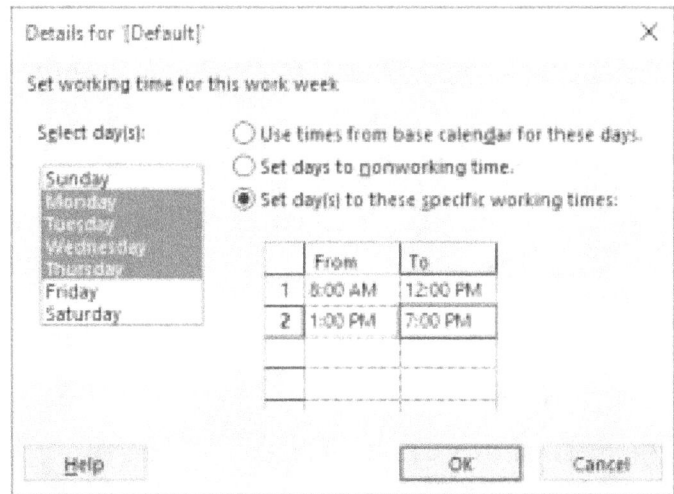

- Click OK to close the Change Working Time dialog box after you've finished making changes to the work week.

For a set amount of time, you can have a separate, non-default working week. For just one month, for instance, you can configure a resource to work four 10-hour days every week. Click below [Default] on the Work Weeks tab, then enter the period's name and start and end times. To modify the working days and hours as previously mentioned in this process, click Details.

HOW TO GIVE A RESOURCE A DIFFERENT BASE CALENDAR

- Select Change Working Time from the Properties group on the Project tab.
- Choose the desired resource in the For calendar area.
- Choose the desired base calendar in the resource's Base calendar field.

Use the Base Calendar field in the Resource Sheet view to rapidly apply the same base calendar to several resources.

COST RESOURCES FOR SETUP

The cost resource is another kind of resource that you can use in Project. In a plan, a cost resource can be used to show the monetary cost of a task. A cost resource's only function is to link a specific kind of expense to one or more tasks, even though work resources (people and equipment) can have related costs (hourly rates and fixed prices per assignment). Travel, entertainment, and training are examples of common cost resource kinds that may be included in a plan for accounting or financial reporting purposes.

Cost resources are ineffective and have little bearing on how a task is scheduled. Cost resources are exempt from the Max. Units, Standard and Overtime pay rate, and Cost Per Use parameters. You can view the cumulative costs for a certain type of cost resource, like the overall travel expenses for a project, after you assign a cost resource to a task and set the cost amount per task.

Compared to work resources, cost resources produce cost values in a different manner. The cost of a work resource can be determined by a pay rate (e.g., $40 per hour for the duration of the assignment), a fixed cost per use (e.g., $100 per assignment), or both. As explained in the subject "Enter work resource pay rates" earlier in this chapter, you only need to set up these pay rates and cost-per-use amounts once for the work resource. But only when you assign a cost resource to a task do you enter its cost value. This can be done in the Task form's Cost field with the Cost detail displayed, or in the Cost field of the Assign Resources dialog box.

HOW TO INCLUDE A COST RESOURCE

- Select Resource Sheet from the Resource Views group on the View tab.

- To add the cost resource, click on the Resource Name column in the Resource Sheet view.
- Click Add Resources in the Insert group on the Resource tab, followed by Cost Resource.

For the new cost resource, the project adds a row. The new cost resource is named <New Resource> in the project.

- Type the name of the cost resource while <New Resource> is chosen, and then hit Enter.

For instance, it is wise to highlight in a note if a resource possesses adaptable talents that can benefit the project. In this manner, the note is part of the plan and is easily readable or printable.

To create a task note, click the Notes button in the Properties group on the **Task tab**. The Notes button on the Resource tab, in the Properties group, is a comparable method for entering resource notes. An additional choice can easily enter notes in the display of the Resource Form. You can browse and edit notes for many resources more quickly when you use the Resource Form.

FILLING OUT THE RESOURCE INFORMATION DIALOG BOX WITH A RESOURCE NOTE

- Select Resource Sheet from the Resource Views group on the View tab.
- Choose a name for the resource.
- Select Notes under the Properties category on the Resource tab.
- Write a note about the resource in the Notes box.

USING THE RESOURCE FORM TO ADD A NOTE FOR A RESOURCE

- Select Resource Sheet from the Resource Views group on the View tab.
- Click the Details button in the Properties group on the Resource tab.

In this kind of split view, the lower pane displays information about the object (in this case, a resource) that is selected in the top pane. By clicking a resource name directly or by selecting Previous or Next in the Resource Form, you can easily change the resource name that is currently selected in the upper pane.

The Schedule information are shown first in the Resource Form view, but it can show any number of details.

- To shift the attention to the Resource Form, click anywhere in the Resource Form view. The Format tab's name is changed to Resource Form Tools.
- Select Notes under the Details group on the Format tab.

Additionally, you can right-click on the Resource Form view's gray background area and select Notes from the shortcut menu that displays. The Resource Form view displays the Notes details. For rapidly adding, modifying, or examining resource details like notes, this split view is excellent.

- Type the resource's note into the Notes field.

You'll notice that the Previous and Next buttons switch to OK and Cancel as soon as you begin composing the note.

- Press OK.

TO ASSIGN A WORK RESOURCE TO A TASK

You can conduct the following steps in most task-centric views that include a table. Examples include the Gantt Chart, Task Sheet, and Task Usage views.

- Click the task to which you want to assign a resource.
- Select Assign Resources from the Assignments group on the Resource tab. The dialog box for

assigning resources opens. You can drag it anywhere you like on the screen.

- Select the resource or resources you wish to assign in the Assign Resources dialog box's Resource Name column, and then select Assign.

Or

In any task-centric view where the Entry table is visible, you can take the following actions.

- Select a task by clicking in the Resource Names column, then click the arrow that shows up. The names of the resources are listed.

Drag the vertical divider bar to the right in a Gantt chart view if the Resource Names column isn't already visible.

- Click the Enter key after checking the box for the resource or resources you wish to assign to the chosen task in the list of resource names.

The Task Form view and the Resources tab of the Task Information dialog box are two additional locations where you can assign resources in addition to the ways that are displayed here. You'll probably find that your preferred method of allocating resources changes as you use Project.

USING THE TASK FORM VIEW TO EXAMINE OR MODIFY ASSIGNMENT DETAILS

These actions can be carried out in any Gantt chart view, including the Task Sheet or Task Usage view.

- Click the Details check box in the Split View group on the View tab. With the Task Form view in the bottom pane, Project divides the window into two panes.
- Click anywhere in the Task Form view. With the focus on the Task Form, note that the label of the Format tab changes to Task Form Tools. Now the commands provided on the Format tab apply to the Task Form.
- On the Format tab, in the Details group, select Work. The Work specifics show in the Task Form.

CONTROL WORK WHEN ADDING OR WITHDRAWING RESOURCE ASSIGNMENTS

As you saw previously, you define the amount of work that a task represents when you initially assign one or more resources to it. For tasks that are automatically (as opposed to manually) planned, Project gives you an option that allows you to determine how it should compute work on a task when you allocate more resources to or unassign resources from the task.

This option is called effort-driven scheduling, and when it is in effect, it operates like this: The labor of a task remains consistent as you assign or unassign resources.

As more resources are assigned to a task, its time decreases. The total work remains the same and is dispersed among the allotted resources.

In a similar vein, a task's duration grows as resources are removed. Distributed across the remaining allotted resources, the overall amount of work stays constant. You can use effort-driven scheduling anyway you see fit. For every task you create in Project, effort-driven scheduling is turned off by default. Effort-driven scheduling can be activated for a whole plan or for individual tasks. Additionally, you can manage how Project recalculates work on a task immediately after assigning or unassigning a resource by using the settings in an Actions list (explained later in this topic).

When effort-driven scheduling is disabled, adding a resource to a task results in more work being done in the same amount of time. Project updates the assignment values and adds more work to this task because effort-driven scheduling is disabled.

When adding or removing resources from a task, you can manage how Project schedules the work using the Actions list. Take note of the tiny green triangle in task 5's upper-left corner. This is a graphical indicator that an action is now available. Until you perform another action, you can use the Actions list to choose how you want Project to handle the additional resource assignment.

In task-centric views with tables, actions indicators show up right away after you complete specific actions, like allocating or releasing resources. Although you can carry out some of the same tasks in the Task Forms, doing so won't cause the Actions indicators to light up. You can see the Actions indication as soon as you switch resource assignments.

You can select the desired scheduling outcome by using these options. You can change the assignment units, the resources' work, or the task's duration.

ADVICE

While using Project, additional Actions indicators will be visible to you. Usually, they show up when you may otherwise wonder, "Why did Project just do that?" (For instance, when you allocate a new resource and the task's duration changes). You can modify how Project reacts to your activities by using the activities list. You can also utilize the Actions list to tell Project how to schedule the remaining resource assignments on a task when it has multiple resources assigned and you remove one of them.

When you remove a resource from a task, you may manage how Project reschedules the remaining assignments using the Actions list. As you add or remove resources from tasks, we have so far concentrated on modifying duration and work values. You can also adjust the default configuration for a task such that as you add resources to the task, its work is unchanged and duration is decreased.

The Task Form additionally conveys the selected task's effort-driven scheduling status. Take note of the outcome after effort-driven scheduling is activated and a different resource is allocated to the task. When effort-driven scheduling is enabled, assigning an additional resource to a task has a different outcome

You might modify Project's response to the additional resource assignment using the Actions list if this wasn't the scheduling outcome you were hoping for. When effort-driven scheduling is on, the sequence in which you perform your tasks is important. When two resources are first assigned to a task that will take three days to complete (that is, twenty-four working hours), the project schedules each resource to work twenty-four hours, for a total of forty-eight hours on the assignment. On the other hand, you might add a second resource after first allocating one to a 24-hour assignment. In this instance, Project will use effort-driven scheduling to arrange for each resource to spend 12 hours concurrently, resulting in a total of 24 hours of work on the assignment. Keep in mind that effort-driven scheduling only modifies task duration when you add or remove resources from a task once it is activated.

When you add more resources to a task, the timetable outcome changes. These actions can be carried out in any task-centric view that has a table. The Gantt Chart, Task Sheet, and Task Usage views are a few examples.

- Choose a task for which a resource or resources have already been assigned.
- Select the desired resource in the Assign Resources dialog box, then click Assign.

- Choose the desired scheduling outcome by clicking the Actions button that shows up immediately to the left of the task name.

ADVICE

The Actions button will also appear when you make changes to assignments in the Resource name column. Only automatically scheduled tasks will display this.

HOW TO ALTER THE SCHEDULE OUTCOME WHEN A TASK'S RESOURCE IS REMOVED

As long as there is still at least one resource allocated to the task, these procedures are applicable. These actions can be carried out in any task-centric view that has a table.

- Choose a task that requires a variety of resources.
- Click the desired assigned resource in the Assign Resources dialog box, and then select Remove.
- Choose the desired scheduling outcome by clicking the Actions button that shows up immediately to the left of the task name.

ADVICE

Unassigning all of a task's resources will prevent the Actions button from showing up. Because work is the outcome of allocating a resource to a task, the Actions button is only applicable when a task has work.

HOW TO OVERSEE THE SCHEDULING OF AN EFFORT-DRIVEN ACTIVITY OR TASKS

- Choose the task or tasks you wish to do.
- Click Information in the Properties group on the Task tab.
- In the Task Information dialog box's Advanced tab, choose or remove the Box for Effort Driven.

All new tasks in a plan should have effort-driven scheduling enabled.

- Select the Options option from the File tab.
- Click Schedule in the Project Options dialog box.
- The New Tasks Are Effort Driven check box should be selected under Scheduling Options For This Project.

ASSIGN TASKS TO COST RESOURCES

Expense categories that you wish to manage and budget for accounting or financial reporting purposes may be included in cost resources. Cost resources don't work and don't affect a task's scheduling because they don't incur assignment units. Actually, no matter how the task's scheduling is altered—for example, by assigning or removing work resources or altering the task's duration—the cost value obtained from allocating a cost resource to a task will stay constant.

In general, the expenses that tasks may result in include: Work resource costs are calculated by multiplying an employee's regular salary by the quantity of work they do on an assignment. When allocating the cost resources to a task, you input fixed dollar amounts known as cost resource costs. Planned costs are represented by the costs obtained via cost-resource assignments. (In fact, all of the expenses that Project has already estimated in the schedule should be regarded as planned costs, including those that come from allocating work resources to tasks.) If you wish to compare the actual costs with the budget, you can input them later.

TO ALLOCATE A TASK'S COST RESOURCE

- Click the task you wish to allocate a cost resource to in a task-centric view with a table. The Gantt Chart, Task Sheet, and Task Usage views are a few examples.
- Click Assign Resources in the Assignments group on the Resource tab. The dialog box for assigning resources opens. It can be dragged to any location on the screen.

- Click the Cost field for the cost resource you wish to allocate in the allocate Resources dialog box, and then type the assignment's cost value.

Once resources have been assigned, review the plan. There are many specifics in your plan once you have made a list of tasks and allocated resources to them. Although they might not be apparent in the view you have chosen, several of these nuances are crucial to the success of your plan. This subject shows how to view a plan's main indicators in a number of ways. Key indicators of a plan can be viewed in Project in a variety of ways. The following queries can be addressed with the aid of these indicators:

- According to the strategy, who is responsible for what tasks? How long will the project take to finish? What will the price be? The answers to these questions will probably alter over time for many projects. This is why being able to display the current project status immediately is a smart practice. As the project manager, you can stay informed, and the sponsors, other stakeholders, and the resources doing the task can all benefit from the information.

ADVICE

The Timeline, Project Summary task, and Project Statistics

dialog box are excellent locations to view the main indications of a plan, in addition to the views and capabilities covered in this chapter. Two typical queries that may arise following the allocation of resources to tasks in a plan are, "How much will this cost? and "What labor is being done by whom, and when? We'll present aspects in this topic that aid in providing answers to these queries. We will often revisit these and related qualities in subsequent chapters because they are crucial questions for effective project management.

How To verify the expenses for each task in the plan

- Click Other Views, then Task Sheet under the Task Views group on the View tab.
- Click Tables in the Data group on the View tab, and then click Cost. The Entry table is replaced with the Cost table.

TO DETERMINE THE EXPENSES OF EACH RESOURCE IN THE PLAN

- Click Resource Sheet under the Resource Views group on the View tab.
- Click Tables in the Data group on the View tab, and then click Cost. The Entry table is replaced with the Cost table.

HOW TO VIEW RESOURCE ALLOCATION AND ADDITIONAL INFORMATION ORGANIZED BY TASK

- Click Task Usage under the Task Views category on the View tab. It displays the Task Usage view.
- Click Tables in the Data group on the View tab, and then select Summary. The Entry table is replaced with the Summary table.

HOW TO VIEW TASK ASSIGNMENTS AND ADDITIONAL INFORMATION CATEGORIZED BY RESOURCE

- Click Resource Usage under the Resource Views group on the View tab. The view for Resource Usage is displayed.
- Click Tables in the Data group on the View tab, and the select summary. The entry table is replaced with summary table.

CHAPTER SIX

CUSTOMIZE REPORTS, ADD TASKS TO A TIMELINE VIEW, AND ALTER A GANTT CHART VIEW

Views and reports can be copied and printed. Similar to a Microsoft Access database file, a project plan can be thought of as a database of information. Typically, not all of the data in a plan is displayed at once. Rather, you concentrate on the part of the plan that you want to see right now. The most popular methods for viewing or printing a plan's data are views and reports. You can significantly format the data in both situations to suit your requirements.

This chapter explains how to personalize and distribute common project views, such as the Gantt Chart, which is closely linked to project management. Reports are another way to visualize your schedule. In addition to tables, reports can also contain vibrant charts and pictures. There are numerous reports in the project that you can use just as is or alter.

ADVICE

Some of Project's more basic view and report formatting tools are covered in this chapter. This chapter walks you through the steps for adding tasks to a Timeline view, customizing reports, copying and printing views and reports, and creating a Gantt chart view. Personalize the view of a Gantt chart.

When American engineer Henry Gantt created a bar chart that displayed resource usage over time in the early 20th century, the Gantt chart became the standard method for visualizing schedules. The Gantt chart is the most widely used visual representation of a project's timetable or plan. In the field of project management, the Gantt chart is actually a well-liked and well-understood depiction of scheduling data. In Project, a Gantt chart takes center stage in the default display. When working in Project, you will probably be in this view a lot of the time.

ADVICE

Project automatically shows a split view called Gantt with Timeline when you create a new plan.

To designate a different view as the default view for a new plan, you can alter this property. Select the Options option from the File tab. Click General in the Project Options dialog box. Click the desired view in the Default View box. The selected view will show up the next time you make a new plan.

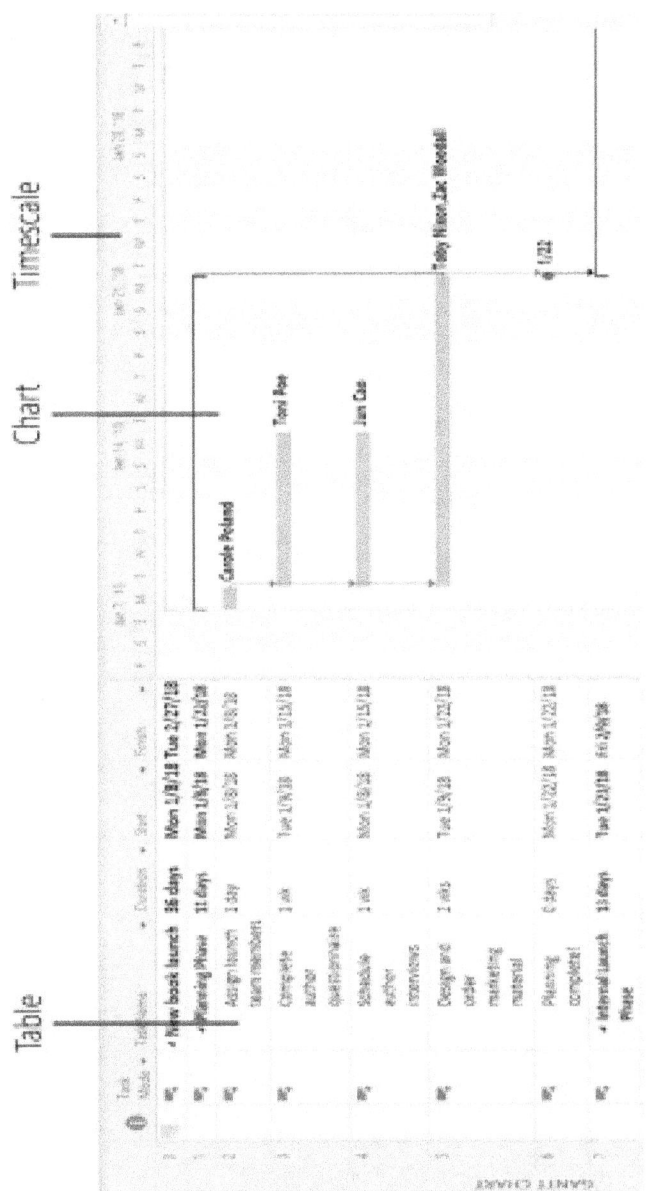

A table on the left and a bar chart with a timeline on the right make up the two primary components of a Gantt chart view. Units of time are shown by an adjustable timeframe band across the top of the bar chart. The tasks in the table are graphically represented by the bars on the chart according to their start and end dates, duration, and status (e.g., whether or not work on the task has begun). Tasks, summary tasks, and milestones are all represented by Gantt bars or symbols on a Gantt chart; each type of bar has a unique format.

Remember that Gantt bars are a representation of tasks in a plan whenever you work with them. Relationships between tasks are represented by other chart elements, including link lines. A Gantt chart view's default formatting is suitable for printing, sharing with other applications, and on-screen viewing. Nevertheless, you can alter the format of practically every Gantt chart element. In a Gantt chart view, the chart elements can be formatted in a number of ways: Apply preset color schemes from the Gantt Chart Style group quickly.

Microsoft Project Bible

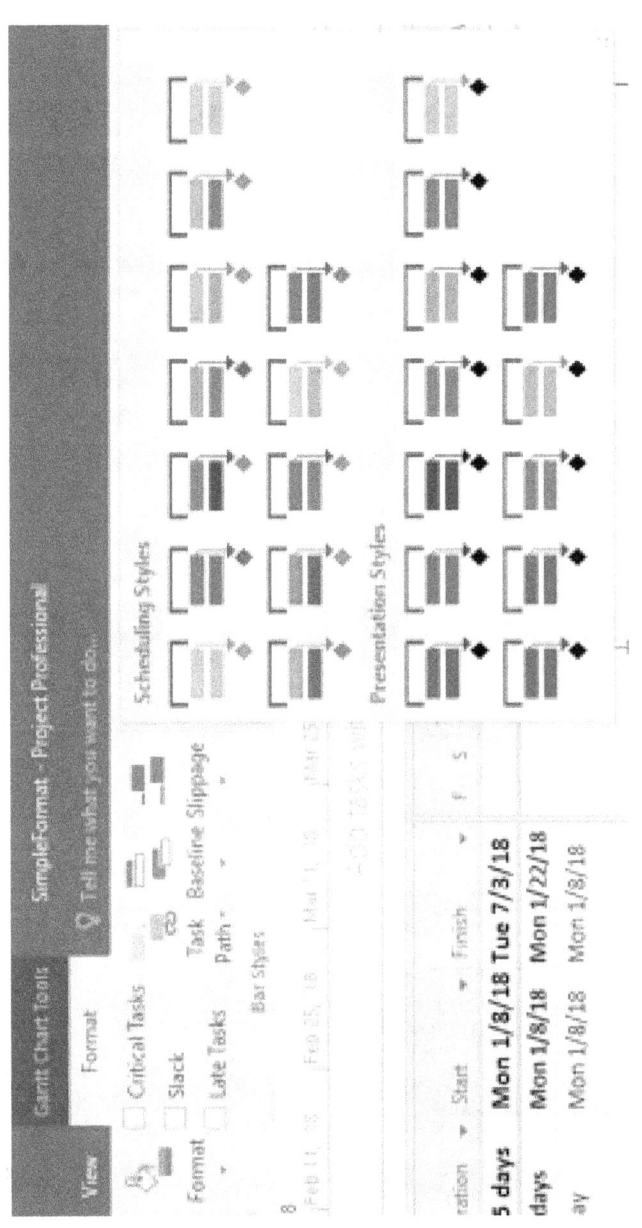

There are two categories for Gantt chart styles:

- Methods of Scheduling Tasks that are scheduled automatically and manually are distinguished by these styles.
- Styles of Presentation: That distinction is not made by these styles. Applying a presentation style to a Gantt chart view is a suitable choice, for example, when displaying a Gantt chart to an audience for whom you do not want to distinguish between activities that are scheduled manually and those that are scheduled automatically. Using the Bar Styles dialog box, apply highly customizable formatting to Gantt bars.

To alter the look of every instance of a certain kind of Gantt bar, use the options on the Bars tab of the Bar Styles dialog box. In this instance, whatever formatting adjustments you make to one kind of Gantt bar—for instance, a summary task—apply to all of the Gantt bars in the Gantt chart. Bar styles are a strong formatting tool that can be applied or customized. Format each Gantt bar separately. Other bars in the Gantt chart are unaffected by the direct formatting adjustments you make. You can format text and cell values in the table section of a Gantt chart view. Project's cell formatting choices are comparable to those found in Microsoft Excel.

HOW TO GIVE GANTT BARS A GANTT CHART APPEARANCE

- Change the view to a Gantt chart.
- To see the preset color styles, click the More button in the Gantt Chart Style group on the Format tab.
- To see every Gantt Chart Style choice available, click the More button.
- Select the desired style by clicking.

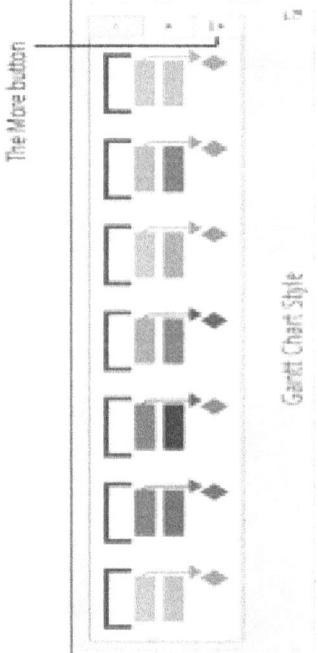

HOW TO FORMAT A UNIQUE GANTT CHART FORM

- Click a Gantt bar twice.

Or

- To format the bar of a task, click on its name. Next, select Format from the Bar Styles category on the Format tab, and then select Bar.
- Choose the desired formatting choices in the Format Bar dialog box.

In order to exclude direct formatting from a specific Gantt bar shape

- Double-click a Gantt chart that has already been formatted.

Or

- On the previously configured Gantt bar, click the task name. Next, select Format from the Bar Styles group on the Format tab, followed by Bar.
- Select Reset from the Format Bar dialog box. To format a range of cells or a single cell.

- Choose the cell or range of cells you wish to format in the table section of a Gantt chart view.
- Choose the desired formatting settings from the Font group on the Task tab.

Or

- Decide which cell or group of cells to format.
- Use the right-click menu to choose a cell or group of cells. A menu with shortcuts is displayed.
- To view the shortcut menu and Mini Toolbar, right-click a table cell, such as one that has a task name.

  Note that the Mini Toolbar shows in addition to the standard shortcut menu.
- Choose your preferred text or cell background formatting options from the Mini Toolbar.

HOW TO GET RID OF EVERY FORMATTING THAT HAS BEEN PUT ON A CELL

- Choose the cell or range of cells that has already been formatted.
- Click Clear (the button that resembles an eraser) and then click Clear Formatting in the Editing group on the Task tab.

To modify the timeline in a Gantt chart view. Take one of the actions listed below:

- Click Timescale in the Zoom group on the View tab, and then select the option you desire.
- To change the zoom level, use the Zoom Slider located in the status bar's lower-right corner.

Include assignments in a timeline view. The easiest way to show important tasks and plan milestones in a clear and concise manner is with a timeline view. You'll share this view with Microsoft PowerPoint presentations, email messages, and other formats outside of Project (you'll do so later in this chapter). It's particularly useful for communicating brief plans. The Timeline view allows you to include just enough information to effectively communicate your point, particularly to other project participants.

Your "project at a glance" view can be a carefully filled-out Timeline view. Typically, a Timeline view appears above the active view. Even if there are tasks in the plan, the Timeline view is initially blank. You choose how the tasks should appear on a Timeline view by selecting the ones that are already there or adding new ones. Actually, you can show more than one timeline at once, and each one can have its own layout settings and tasks. To include already-completed tasks in a timeline view. In a Timeline view, click anywhere.

ADVICE

Choose the Timeline check box in the Split View group on the View tab if the Timeline is not displayed.

- The Timeline Tools label appears above the Format tab when Project switches to the Timeline view.
- Select Existing Tasks under the Insert group on the Format tab.
- The dialog box to add tasks to the timeline appears. An overview of the plan's summary and subtasks can be seen in this dialog box. In order to exclude direct formatting from a specific Gantt bar shape.
- Double-click a Gantt chart that has already been formatted.

Or

- On the previously configured Gantt bar, click the task name. Next, select Format from the Bar Styles group on the Format tab, followed by Bar.
- Select Reset from the Format Bar dialog box.

HOW TO FORMAT A RANGE OF CELLS OR A SINGLE CELL

- Choose the cell or range of cells you wish to format in the table section of a Gantt chart view.
- Choose the desired formatting settings from the Font group on the Task tab.

Or

- Decide which cell or group of cells to format.
- Use the right-click menu to choose a cell or group of cells. A menu with shortcuts is displayed.

To view the shortcut menu and Mini Toolbar, right-click a table cell, such as one that has a task name. Note that the Mini Toolbar shows in addition to the standard shortcut menu.

- Choose your preferred text or cell background formatting options from the Mini Toolbar.

HOW TO GET RID OF EVERY FORMATTING THAT HAS BEEN PUT ON A CELL

- Choose the cell or range of cells that has already been formatted.

- Click Clear (the button that resembles an eraser) and then click Clear Formatting in the Editing group on the Task tab.

HOW TO MODIFY THE TIMELINE IN A GANTT CHART VIEW

Take one of the actions listed below:

- Click Timescale in the Zoom group on the View tab, and then select the option you desire.
- To change the zoom level, use the Zoom Slider located in the status bar's lower-right corner.

Include assignments in a timeline view. The easiest way to show important tasks and plan milestones in a clear and concise manner is with a timeline view. You'll share this view with Microsoft PowerPoint presentations, email messages, and other formats outside of Project (you'll do so later in this chapter). It's particularly useful for communicating brief plans. The Timeline view allows you to include just enough information to effectively communicate your point, particularly to other project participants.

Your "project at a glance" view can be a carefully filled-out Timeline view. Typically, a Timeline view appears above the active view. Even if there are tasks in the plan, the Timeline view is initially blank. You choose how the tasks should appear on a Timeline view by selecting the ones that are already there or adding new ones. Actually, you can show more than one timeline at once, and each one can have its own layout settings and tasks.

HOW TO INCLUDE ALREADY-COMPLETED TASKS IN A TIMELINE VIEW

- In a Timeline view, click anywhere.
- The Timeline Tools label appears above the Format tab when Project switches to the Timeline view.
- Select Existing Tasks under the Insert group on the Format tab.
- The dialog box to add tasks to the timeline appears. An overview of the plan's summary and subtasks can be seen in this dialog box.

HOW TO SHOW A REPORT

- Select a category from the View Reports group on the Report tab, and then click the desired report.

HOW TO ADD A STYLE TO A REPORT'S CHART

- Show the report with the desired styled chart in it.
- Select any location on the chart.
- Select the desired style from the Chart Styles group on the Chart Tools Design menu.

HOW TO GIVE A TABLE IN A REPORT A STYLE

- Show the report with the table you wish to design included.
- Select any location on the table.
- Select the desired style from the Table Styles group on the Table Tools Design menu.

CHAPTER SEVEN
DUPLICATE REPORTS AND VIEWS

Standard copying and pasting of data, including a variety of task titles and details, is supported by Project via the Clipboard. However, there are situations in which you may wish to communicate your intentions with coworkers who do not have Project or who might prefer a straightforward schedule snapshot. The majority of Project's thoughts and reports are easily replicable. Views and reports that have been copied can then be added to emails, presentations, and other documents. The Team Planner (only available to Project Professionals), Form views (like the Task Form), and the Relationship diagram are among the views that cannot be simply copied from Project.

ADVICE

Use a screen capture tool like the **Windows Snipping Tool** if you need a visual representation of a view or report that cannot be duplicated straight from Project.

Sharing schedule details works nicely with both Gantt charts and Timeline views. The Gantt chart is a popular schedule format, and the Timeline offers a succinct "project at a glance" approach.

Sharing reports with other project stakeholders is another excellent use for them. Reports are particularly useful for presenting the data in charts from your plan that you might otherwise have to make in Excel.

You can choose what is pasted when you copy a Timeline view or any report to a Microsoft Office application. Pasting a graphic image or editable portions of a copied timeline or report is supported by the Office applications.

HOW TO REPLICATE A VIEW

To duplicate a Gantt chart and the majority of other Project views, use this method.

- Configure the view how you would like it to look when duplicated. For instance, you can scroll to see the range of tasks you wish to replicate together with their Gantt bars in a Gantt chart view.

The Gantt bars of the chosen task can be seen by rapidly scrolling the Gantt chart. Click Scroll To Task in the Editing group on the Task tab.

- Click the arrow next to Copy in the Clipboard group on the Task tab, and then select Copy Picture.

The dialog window for copying a picture opens.

PRINT REPORTS AND VIEWS

You can print the majority of views and all reports, as well as share the details of your plan by copying and pasting. The Relationship Diagram and form views are among the views that are not printable.

What you may see on your screen at any given time may be a comparatively modest fraction of a multi-task plan. It can take a lot of paper to print from Project; in fact, some heavy users utilize plotters to print their plans in poster size.

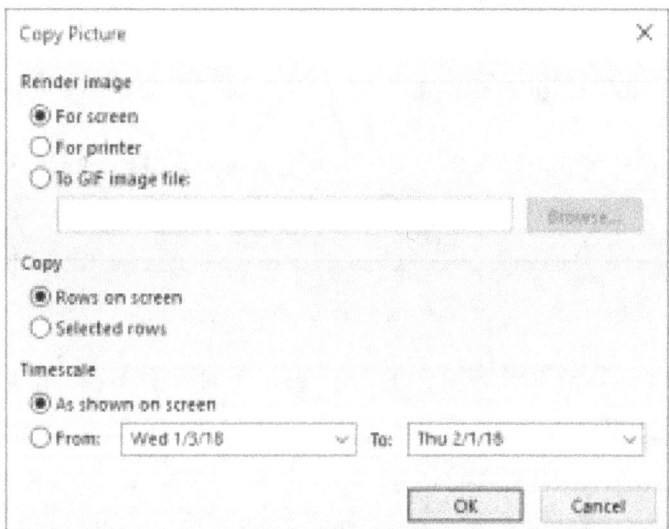

Previewing the views and reports you plan to print is a smart idea, regardless of whether you use a plotter or a printer.

When printing from Project, you can choose to print a particular range of dates on a Gantt chart view, which is covered later in this article. Prior to printing, you may also manage what will print in a view by limiting the display to summary tasks, filtering or collapsing tasks. The Print window is where you work with these settings. This item describes some of the most practical solutions.

Start by using the page navigation buttons located in the screen's lower-right corner. To adjust what is shown, use the page navigation and zoom controls located in the Print window's lower-right corner. You can switch to a multipage view to see a preview of the output in a larger format. The complete view or report will then show up in the Print window. The view or report may be spread across multiple sheets, assuming that you have chosen a letter-sized sheet as your paper size.

You can be choosier when using time-scaled views, such as the Gantt Chart. The preview can be changed to only show the area of the view that spans a given range of dates. You use the Settings to accomplish this.

For instance, you can configure the Print window of a Gantt chart to display only a particular range of dates.

To modify the appearance of a Gantt chart view when printed, use the Print options.

A report may be a more condensed manner of printing information regarding your plan than views. Reports arrange and display data using well recognized formats, like tables and charts.

In Project, printing reports is primarily a "what you see is what you get" process. Project's Report Tools Design tab, which appears when you click in a report, provides a few report-specific printing options.

When you plan to print a report, the Page Breaks command is particularly helpful. Depending on the current page settings, it displays dashed lines in the report to indicate how it will print over pages. As you create your report, you may find the other settings in the Page Setup category, including margins and paper size, helpful.

ADVICE

It is not possible to print certain views from Project, including the relationship diagram and the Form views. However, you can take a screenshot of such a view and print it out using a screen-capture tool like the Windows Snipping Tool.

HOW TO PRINT A VIEW

- Select the view you wish to print from the Task Views group on the View tab.
- Select Print from the File tab.

The preview view is shown beside the Backstage view's Print page.

- Click Print after making your selections.

HOW TO PRINT A REPORT

- Select the report you wish to print from the View Reports group on the Report tab.
- Choose whatever parameters you like from the Page Setup group on the Report Tools Design tab.
- Select Print from the File tab.

The report appears in the preview together with the Print page of the Backstage view.

- After making your selections, click Print.

HOW TO MODIFY A REPORT'S PAGE SETUP PARAMETERS

- Show the report whose page configuration settings you wish to change.
- Select the tab for Report Tools Design.

Take notice of the four commands in the Page Setup group. Take any of these actions:

- Based on the paper size you have chosen, click Page Breaks to view where the page breaks will appear in the report.
- To change the report's page margins when printed, click Margins.
- To change the report's layout from landscape (horizontal) to portrait (vertical), click Orientation.
- To choose the size of your paper, click Size.

MONITOR PROGRESS: FUNDAMENTAL METHODS

Recognize progress tracking Keep a baseline of your strategy. Keep to a plan as planned. Enter the percentage of a task completed. Enter the tasks' real values.

Up until now, you have concentrated on project planning, which is creating and sharing a plan's specifics before to the start of actual work. The next stage of project management, progress tracking, starts when work starts. Tracking entails keeping track of information like who completed what, when, and how much it cost. These specifics are frequently referred to as actuals. Several things occur when you begin tracking task actuals. Project determines the actual and remaining cost, work, and time values as you document your progress on a task. Their summary tasks incorporate these revised values. These modifications are the outcome of the project's dynamic recalculation of the plan.

The steps in this chapter include saving a baseline of your plan, tracking a plan as planned, entering the percentage of a task that has been completed, and entering the actual values for tasks.

RECOGNIZE PROGRESS TRACKING

Rather than only planning a project, effective project management requires tracking actuals. The project manager needs to be aware of the team's performance and know when to make adjustments. The following questions can be addressed by accurately monitoring project performance and contrasting it with the initial plan (as stored in a baseline):

Are things beginning and ending on schedule? If not, how will this affect the project's completion date?

Are resources taking longer or shorter than anticipated to do tasks?

Are unexpectedly high task expenses increasing the project's overall cost?

Will you be able to assess how well you (or the team) estimated in previous projects when planning comparable ones in the future?

There are multiple ways to monitor the project's progress. The degree of control or detail that you, your project sponsor, and other stakeholders require should determine the tracking system you use. It takes more effort on your part and perhaps that of the resources involved in the project to keep track of the minute details. Therefore, you should decide how much detail you require before you start measuring progress.

The following are the various tracking detail levels, arranged from most basic to most extensive:

As planned, document project work. If everything in the project goes according to plan, this level functions at its finest.

Note the proportion of each activity completed, either exactly or in predetermined increments of 25, 50, 75, and 100 percent.

For every task or assignment, note the real start and end dates, the amount of work that has been done thus far, and the duration.

Keep track of tasks at the assignment level throughout time. The most thorough tracking level is this one. Actual work values for each day, week, or other interval are recorded here. You may need to employ a combination of these strategies in a single plan because different project components may have different tracking requirements. For instance, you might want to keep a closer eye on high-risk tasks than low-risk ones.

Keep a baseline of your strategy. As a project manager, one of your most crucial tasks after creating a plan is to document actuals and assess project performance. The planned plan will probably change as you update it or record actuals. Because of this, it is challenging to monitor the plan in its first form.

The start, end, and duration values of a task describe its present "as scheduled" state. The Start, Finish, and Duration sections will change to reflect the task's current status when you add the Actual Start and Actual Finish dates.

Comparing the project's performance to your initial plan will help you assess it accurately. The baseline plan, or simply the baseline, is the name given to this initial strategy. In addition to work and cost values per task, resource, and assignment, saving a baseline also records the initial scheduled start, end, and duration values. Additionally, the baseline contains effort and expense values that are spread out over time; these are known as time-phased values. When comparing what you anticipated happening to what really occurred, use the baseline.

Project captures a snapshot of the current values when you save a baseline, which you may then compare in the future. When you have created the strategy as thoroughly as possible, you should save a baseline. (This does not exclude you from adding assignments, resources, or tasks to the plan once work has begun, though; this is frequently inevitable.)

You haven't started inputting real numbers yet, like the percentage of a task that has been completed. A following baseline (up to 11 per plan) is what you wish to preserve.

Along with time-phased fields, a baseline saves specified values in a number of task, resource, and assignment fields. The project enables up to 11 baselines in a single plan, rather than just one. Baseline is the first one, and Baselines 1 through 10 are the others. For projects with particularly lengthy planning stages, when you may wish to compare various sets of baseline data, saving numerous baselines can be helpful. As the planning details change, for instance, you may wish to save and compare the baseline plans each month. Alternatively, you may want to store a fresh baseline at different stages of the project's execution.

For instance, Baseline might be saved prior to the start of work, Baseline 1 a month later, Baseline 2 two months later, and so forth. After that, you can examine the different baselines and contrast them with the project's actual timeline.

The variance table is an excellent tool for displaying the baseline and scheduled values for tasks side by side for convenient comparison. One excellent method for comparing the scheduled and baseline values of tasks is to display the variance table. Take a plan, for instance, where the start and finish dates are "as scheduled" dates. Due to actuals that did not match the baseline dates or other schedule modifications made by the project manager, they may deviate from the baseline start and finish dates.

The Gantt Chart view can also be formatted to display baseline Gantt bars. On the chart section of a Gantt chart view, a baseline Gantt bar shows the task's baseline start, end, and duration values.

to maintain a baseline.

- Click Set Baseline in the Schedule category on the Project tab, and then click Set Baseline. The dialog box for setting the baseline opens.

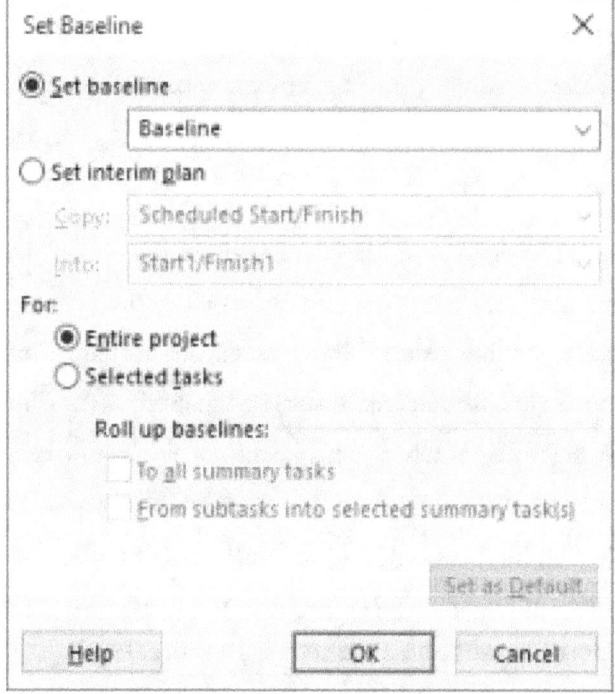

- Click Set Baseline and choose Baseline from the list to preserve the plan's initial baseline.

Or

- Click Set Baseline and choose the desired baseline number to save a subsequent baseline.
- Press OK.

Despite the fact that the Gantt Chart view shows no signs of change, the project saves the baseline.

HOW TO REMOVE A BASELINE THAT HAS ALREADY BEEN SAVED

- Click Set Baseline and then Clear Baseline in the Schedule category on the Project tab.
- Click OK after making your selections in the Clear Baseline dialog box.

In a Gantt chart view, to show baseline Gantt bars

- Click Baseline in the Bar Styles category on the Format tab of a Gantt chart view. Next, click the baseline (Baseline or Baseline1 through Baseline10) that you wish to show.
- For the baseline you select, Project creates baseline Gantt charts.

HOW TO USE THE VARIANCE TABLE TO SHOW SCHEDULED AND BASELINE VALUES

- Select Other Views under the Task Views group on the View tab, and then select Task Sheet.

The view of the Task Sheet opens. There is more space to view the table's fields because this is a tabular view and does not include a Gantt chart.

- Select Tables under the Data group on the View tab.
- Select Variance.

ADVICE

To go to a different table, you can simply right-click the Select All button located in the top-left corner of the active table.

Reporting that the actual task is going exactly as planned is the simplest way to monitor progress. For instance, you may immediately note in the Update Project dialog box that all of the tasks in a five-week project have begun and completed on time if the first week has passed.

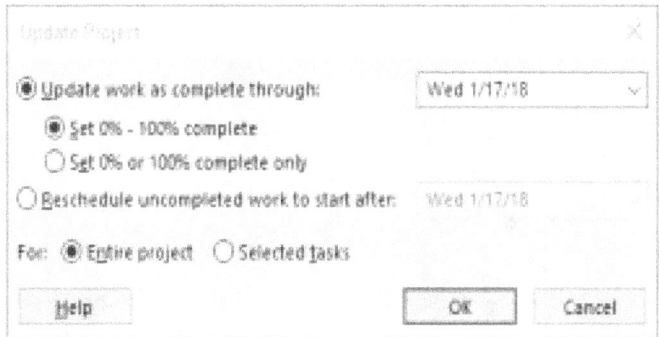

HOW TO ALTER THE KIND OF TASK-TO-TASK RELATIONSHIP

- Decide which successor task you wish to modify.
- To access the Task Information dialog box, which includes information about the task that is now chosen, click the Information button in the Properties group on the Task tab.

To quickly open the Task Information dialog box, double-click a task name.

- Select the tab for Predecessors.
- Choose the desired relationship type between the tasks in the Type column of the predecessor task on the Predecessors tab, and then click OK.
- To exit the Task Information dialog box, click OK.

HOW TO INCREASE THE LEAD TIME OR LAG TIME BETWEEN RELATED TASKS

- Decide which successor task you wish to add lead or lag time to.
- Click the Information button in the Properties group on the Task pane.

Select the Predecessors tab in the Task Information dialog box, and then take one of the following actions:

- Type the desired lead value in the Lag field for a predecessor task. Negative lag values are used to enter lead values. Lead can be expressed as a percentage of the previous task's duration (e.g., -25%) or as a number of working days (e.g., -2d).
- Enter the desired lag value in the Lag field for a predecessor task. Lag values are input as positive numbers. Lag can be expressed as a percentage of the previous task's time (e.g., 50%) or as a number of working days (e.g., 3d).

HOW TO USE RESTRICTIONS TO MANAGE THE SCHEDULING OF TASKS

There are constraints of some kind attached to every task you enter into Project. The extent to which an automatically scheduled work can be postponed depends on a constraint.

The intricacies of the constraints on automatically scheduled tasks are manageable. However, you are unable to alter the constraint type or specify a constraint date when working with a manually scheduled task. The rationale is that limitations have no effect because Project does not manually schedule tasks.

Constraints fall into three categories:

- Flexible Constraints
- Semi-flexible constraint
- Inflexible constraint

FLEXIBLE CONSTRAINTS

A project may alter a task's start and end dates. Tasks begin as soon as possible because of the project's default constraint type. As Soon As Possible, or ASAP for short, is the name given to this kind of flexible restriction. Flexible constraints have no linked constraint date. In the Indicators column for flexible constraints, the project does not show any unique indicators.

SEMI-FLEXIBLE CONSTRAINT

A task that is subject to this kind of constraint has a start or finish date boundary. Nonetheless, Project offers the scheduling flexibility to alter a task's start and end dates within that range. Take, for instance, a task that has a deadline of March 10, 2024, but has the potential to be completed earlier. Soft constraints or mild constraints are other names for semi-flexible constraints.

In the Indicators column, Project shows a unique constraint indicator that resembles a calendar when a task has been subjected to a semi-flexible constraint.

INFLEXIBLE CONSTRAINT

This kind of constraint requires that a task start or finish on a specific date. You can stipulate, for instance, that a work must be completed by March 10, 2024. Hard restrictions are another name for inflexible limitations. Project shows a constraint indicator in the Indicators column when a task has been subjected to an inflexible constraint. The constraint details can be seen in a ScreenTip by pointing to a constraint indicator. To view the details of the limitation, use the ScreenTip.

The following table lists the eight different categories of task limitations. Task scheduling is impacted differently by these three types of constraints:

FLEXIBLE CONSTRAINT

The project's start date (for ASAP task constraints) or end date (for As Late As Possible [ALAP] task constraints) are the only restrictions on how tasks can be planned. As soon as possible (ASAP) and successor relationships are examples of these constraints. These constraint types do not enforce start or end dates. Whenever feasible, use these constraint kinds.

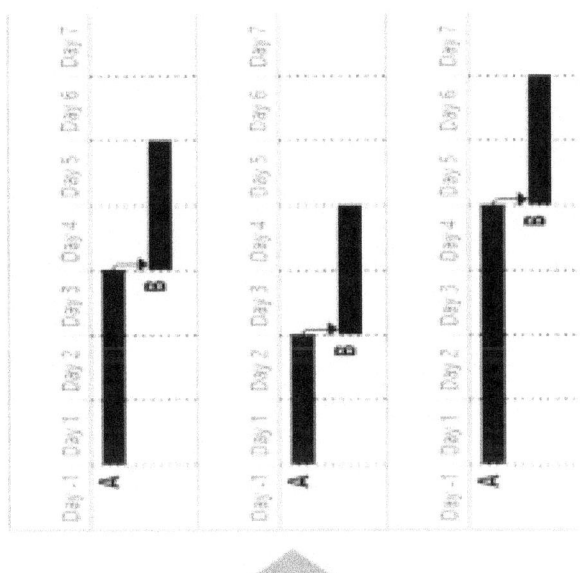

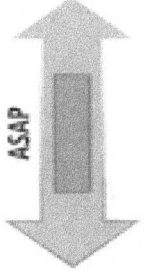

Take, for instance, a schedule where activities A and B are connected and task B is subject to an ASAP restriction. The start date of task B is automatically modified to reflect changes in task A's length.

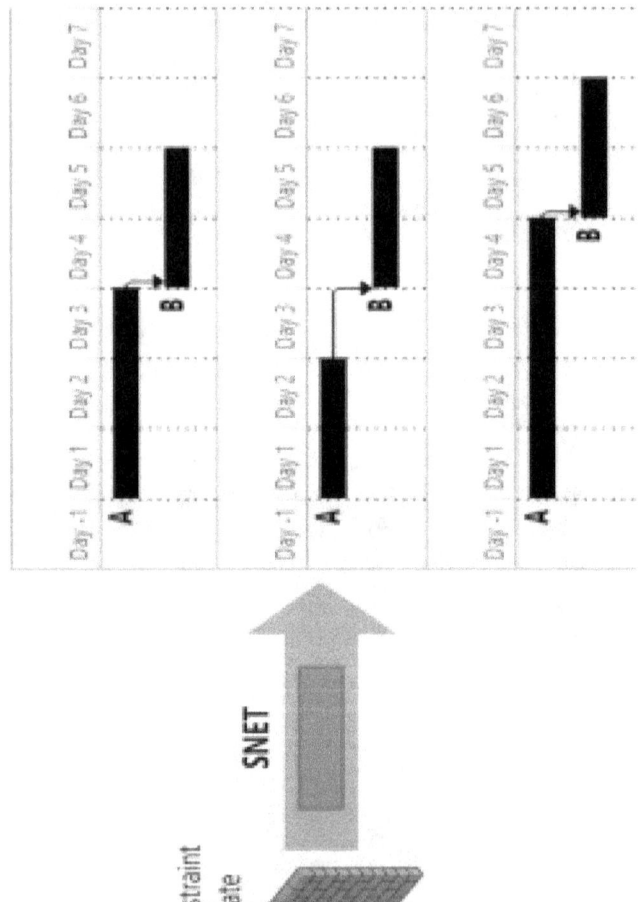

SEMI-FLEXIBLE RESTRICTIONS

These restrictions, like Start No Earlier Than or Start No Later Than (SNET or SNLT), restrict how many times a task can be rescheduled within the given time frame.

Tasks A and B are connected, and task B has a SNET constraint set to day 4 with a SNET constraint of some kind. The beginning of task B remains unchanged if task A takes less time. However, Project automatically modifies the start date of task B if work A takes longer than expected.

INFLEXIBLE CONSTRAINT

These limitations, such Must Start On (MSO), make it impossible to reschedule a work. These constraint types should only be used in dire circumstances. Without any scheduling flexibility, a Must Start On (MSO) restriction "pins" a task's start date to a particular date. Tasks A and B are connected in this example, and task B's MSO restriction is set at day 4. The beginning of task B is unaffected by changes in task A's duration.

Jason Taylor

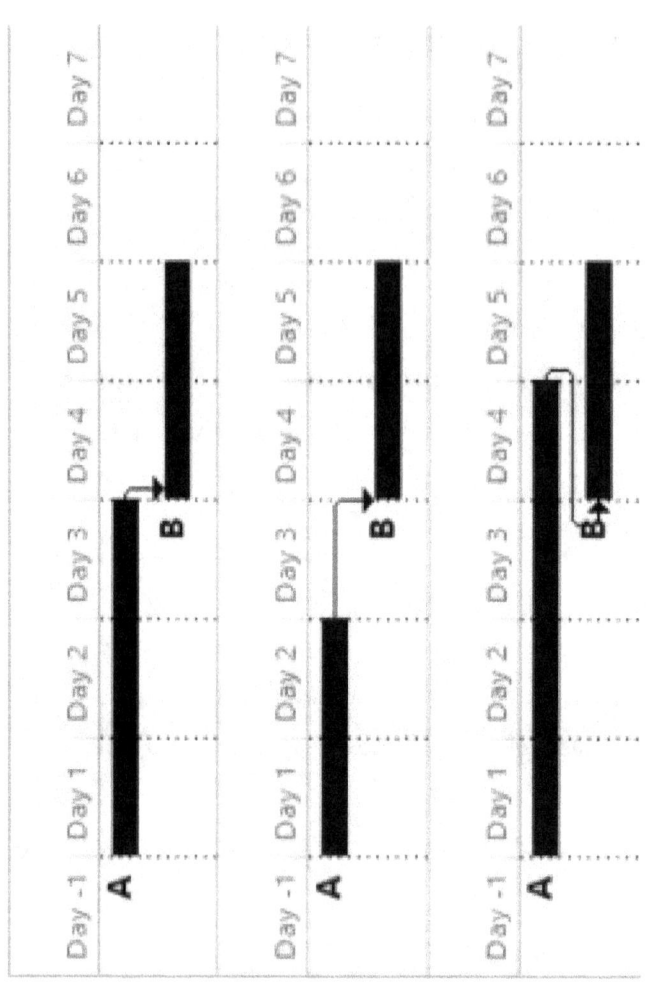

What you require from the project will determine the kind of constraint you apply to the activities in your plans. Only when a task's start or conclusion date is set by circumstances outside the project team's control should you employ rigid limits. Handoffs to clients and the conclusion of a funding cycle are two examples of such tasks. You should use flexible constraints for tasks that don't have these restrictions. The most flexibility in modifying start and end dates is offered by flexible restrictions, which also enable Project to modify dates in the event that your strategy changes. For instance, Project modifies, or pulls in, the start and end dates of all successor tasks if you apply ASAP restrictions and the predecessor task's duration goes from four to two days. However, the project cannot change the start or end dates of a successor task if an inflexible constraint is applied.

When imposing limitations on work, bear the following points in mind:

When a task's completion date is entered (for instance, in the Finish column), a Finish No Earlier Than constraint is applied to the task.

A Start No Earlier Than constraint is applied to a task when a Start date is entered (for instance, in the Start column) or a

Gantt bar is dragged directly on the Gantt chart. Entering a deadline date is frequently a better option than entering a semi-constraint that is either flexible or rigid.

Project uses the Default Start Time or Default End Time value that is set on the Schedule tab of the Project Options dialog box to schedule the start or finish time of a constraint date unless you specify a time. (Click the File tab to bring up the Background view, and then click Options to open this dialog box.) 8:00 a.m. is the start time by default. Enter the start date and time if you would want a confined task to be scheduled to begin at a different time. For instance, type 5/12/24 10AM in the Start field to set a task to begin.

You may develop what is known as negative slack if you have to impose semi-flexible or stiff constraints to tasks in addition to task linkages. Assume, for instance, that a task that comes after you has a finish-to-start link with its predecessor. There is negative slack and a scheduling conflict if you enter a Must Start On constraint for the successor task before the predecessor task's completion date. The relationship is overridden by the constraint date that is applied to the successor task by default. You can, however, configure Project to prioritize relationships above limitations if you'd like. Clear the Tasks Will Always Honor

Their Constraint Dates check box on the Schedule tab of the Project Options dialog box to accomplish this. Certain constraint behaviors are different if you have to schedule a project from a finish date instead of a start date. For new tasks, for instance, the default constraint type is As Late As Possible instead of As Soon As Possible. When scheduling from a finish date, you should be very aware of the limitations to ensure that you get the desired impact.

- To apply a task constraint, first choose the task name that has to be restricted.
- The task needs to be scheduled automatically; manually planned tasks are not subject to task limitations.
- Click the Information button in the Properties group on the Task pane.

Tip: To quickly open the Task Information dialog box, double-click a task name.

- Select the Advanced tab in the Task Information dialog box.
- Choose the desired constraint type in the Constraint Type box.
- With the exception of As Soon As Possible and As Late As Possible, all constraint types call for a

limit date. Click OK after entering or choosing the desired date in the Constraint Date box.

HOW TO GET RID OF A TASK RESTRICTION

- Pick a task that has been subjected to a constraint.
- Click the Information button in the Properties group on the Task pane.
- Select the Advanced tab in the Task Information dialog box.
- Choose As Soon As Possible or, if scheduling from the project completion date, As Late As Possible in the Constraint Type box.

You may have anticipated that work on a certain task would be stopped when you first planned the project's duties. You can divide a task into two or more parts rather than listing it twice to accommodate a known **work stoppage**. You may want to divide a task for the reasons listed below: You expect a task to be interrupted. This could occur, for instance, if the location where a task needs to be completed is inaccessible halfway through the activity's duration. Unexpectedly, a task is interrupted. A resource may have to cease working on a task once it has started because another issue has gained precedence. The resource can get back to work on the task once the other problem has been fixed. To divide a task into several parts, drag the mouse pointer inside a Gantt bar. Divide a task to accommodate for a work interruption. In Gantt chart views, Project creates a dotted line between the two task segments when you split the work. When dividing up responsibilities, bear the following points in mind:

- To reschedule a split task, drag a section of it to the left or right.

The task's duration does not include the time spent on the task split, which is indicated by the dotted line. There is no work done during the split. By checking the Show Bar Splits check box in the Layout dialog box, you can choose to hide the dotted line between segments. (Clicking the Layout button in the Format group on the Format tab will open this dialog box.). When a split task's duration varies, the final portion of the task is adjusted correspondingly. The entire task gets rescheduled, splits and all, if a split task is rescheduled (for instance, if its start date changes). The task maintains the same divides and segments. Tasks may split as a result of resource leveling or manual contoured assignments over time.

CHAPTER EIGHT

HOW TO DIVIDE A TASK

To divide a task into many parts:

- Choose the task name and then click Scroll to Task in the Editing group on the Task tab if the task's Gantt bar is not displayed in the chart section of the Gantt chart view.
- To display a ScreenTip and switch the mouse cursor to task-splitting mode, click the Split Task button (which resembles a broken Gantt bar) in the Schedule group on the Task tab.
- Drag the mouse pointer over the task's Gantt bar without clicking until the desired split's beginning shows in the ScreenTip.
- Drag the mouse pointer to the right after clicking until the desired start date for the new segment shows in the ScreenTip. Let go of the mouse button.

ADVICE

You can undo the split (by pressing Ctrl+Z) and try again if the first attempt doesn't yield the desired outcome to postpone a split task 1's second part. Drag the task's second or subsequent segment to the desired new start date.

Dragging a split task's first segment will cause the task to be rescheduled and add a SNET constraint. Drag the second, not the first, part of a split task to change the split between the first and second segments. Reuniting two halves of a divided task

- Drag one task section until it makes contact with the other part.

ADAPT WORKING HOURS TO SPECIFIC TASKS

On occasion, you may wish a certain task to take place at a time other than the project calendar's working hours. Or maybe you want a task to take place at a time that is different from the resource's calendar-based regular working hours. You apply a task calendar to these tasks in order to achieve this. You designate the base calendar to use as a task calendar, just like you would with the project calendar.

The following are instances in which a task calendar may be necessary:

- You have a task that needs to be completed overnight, and you are utilizing the Standard base calendar as your project calendar. Your regular working hours are 8:00 a.m. to 5:00 p.m.
- You have a task that needs to be completed on a particular weekday. You have an assignment that

needs to be completed over the weekend. Project does not generate calendars when you create tasks, which is how it handles tasks differently than resources. A base calendar is assigned to the task when a task calendar is required. This foundation calendar could be one that comes with Project or one that you make yourself.

Creating a new calendar by cloning the Standard base calendar has the advantage of displaying all of the working-day exceptions—like holidays—that you have previously placed in the Standard calendar. However, neither calendar is impacted by any future modifications made to the other.

Project schedules operate throughout the regular working hours shared by the task calendar and resource calendars for projects that contain both schedules. When you apply the task calendar or allocate a resource to a task, Project notifies you if there isn't a standard working hour. You have the option to disregard resource calendars for every resource linked to the task when you apply a task calendar to it. Project will then schedule the resources to work on the task in accordance with the task calendar rather than their own resource calendars (e.g., to work twenty-four hours a day).

In order to make a fresh foundation calendar

- To access the Change Working Time dialog box, click the Change Working Time button in the Properties group on the Project tab.
- Click Create New Calendar in the Change Working Time dialog box to bring up the Create New Base Calendar dialog box.

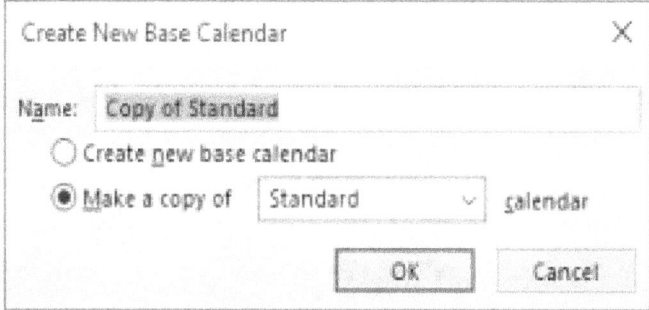

Make sure the name you choose for your new basic calendar makes sense to everyone who uses it.

- Type the new base calendar's name into the Name box, and then do one of the following actions:
- Click Create new base calendar to create a new calendar with working hours of 8:00 AM to 5:00 PM, Monday through Friday.
- Click the Make a copy of option, then choose the base calendar you wish to use from the list to create

167

a new calendar that initially corresponds to an existing base calendar.
- Press OK.
- In the Change Working Time dialog box, under the Exceptions and Work Weeks tabs, enter the specific working time exceptions or global changes you wish to make for this calendar in order to enter the working-time details for this new calendar.
- To exit the Change Working Time dialog box, click OK.

TO ASSIGN A TASK TO A BASE CALENDAR
- Choose the task name that you wish to use with the base calendar.
- To access the Task Information dialog box, click the Information button in the Properties group on the Task tab.
- Select the tab for Advanced.
- Choose the base calendar from the list of available base calendars in the Calendar box.

Microsoft Project Bible

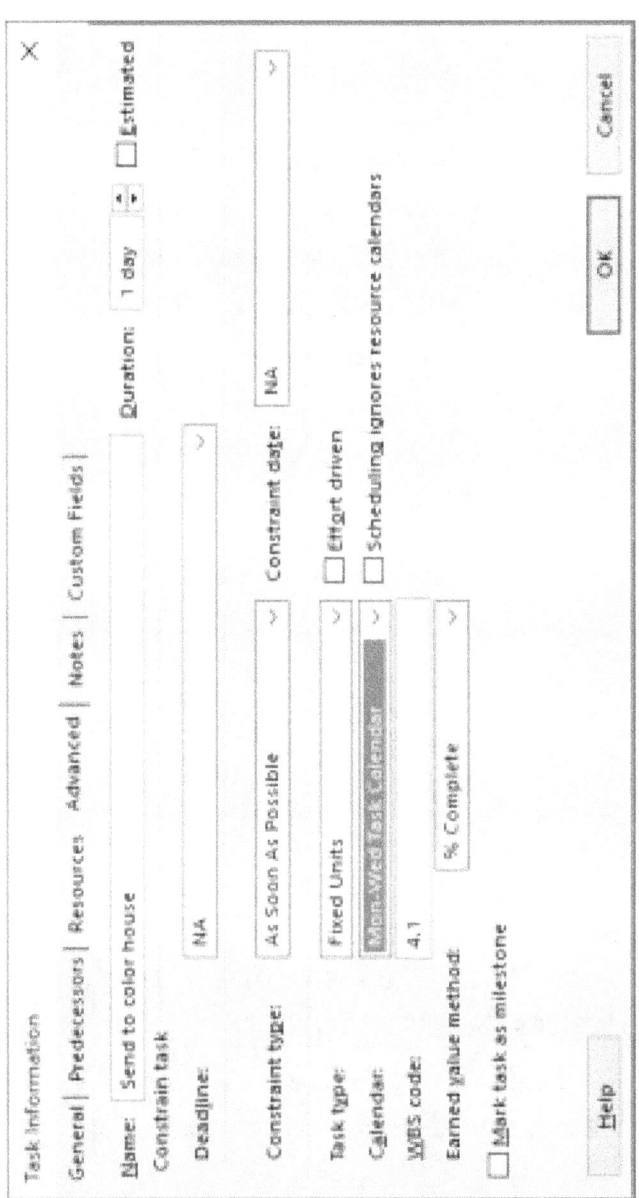

To apply a base calendar to a task, use the Calendar field in the Task Information dialog box.

- To exit the dialog box, click OK. The base calendar is the task calendar for this task, and the project applies it to the task. To remind you that this work has a task calendar applied to it, a calendar icon shows up in the Indicators column.
- Point to the calendar icon to view the calendar details. The calendar details are displayed via a ScreenTip.

To view the name of the calendar, use the ScreenTip.

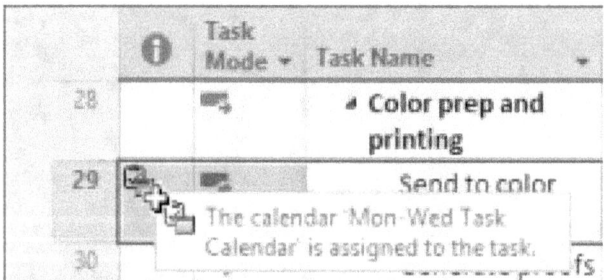

TO UTILIZE COLUMN HEADINGS TO FILTER ACTIVITIES OR RESOURCES

- Present a view with a table that is task- or resource-centric. The Resource Sheet view and the Gantt chart are two excellent examples.

- If required, navigate to the table containing the value you wish to sort by clicking Tables in the Data group on the View tab, and then choose the desired table.
- Select the column heading that you wish to filter by clicking the arrow to the right of it.

Choose from the following options in the menu that displays:

- To pick only the values you wish to have shown, click pick All to remove all of the values listed.
- Depending on the type of field, select Filters if it is available, and then either apply a filter or create a custom AutoFilter.

HOW TO MAKE OR MODIFY A FILTER

- Show the view that you wish to filter.
- Click More Filters to open the More Filters dialog box after selecting the Filter arrow in the Data group on the View tab.

Take one of these actions:

- To start from scratch when creating a new filter, click New.
- To make changes to an existing filter, select it and click Edit.

- Click Copy to build a new filter based on an existing filter after selecting an existing filter.

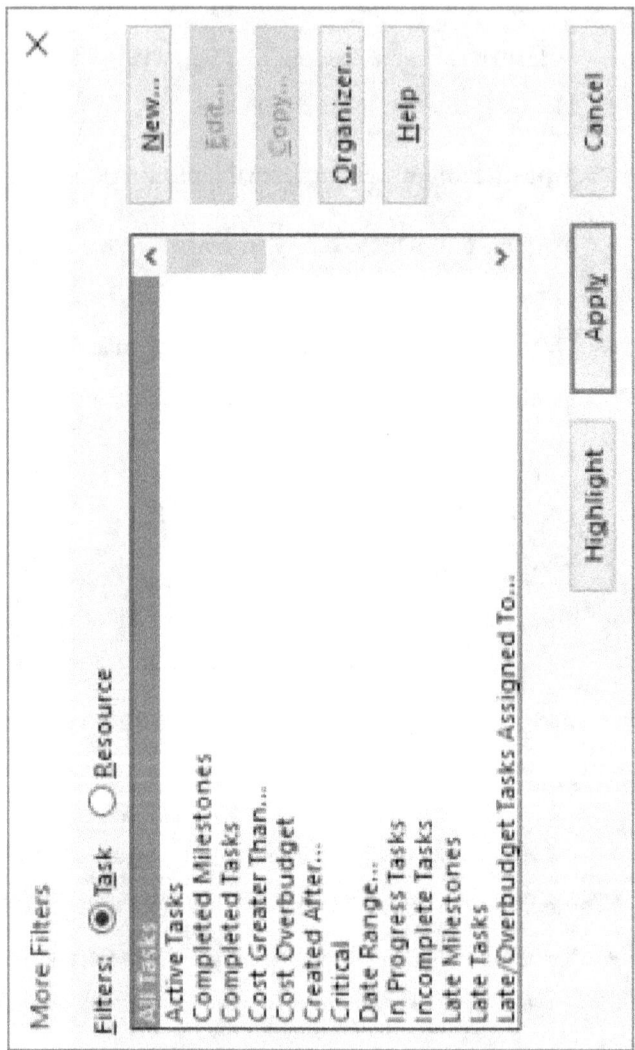

You can edit a duplicate of an existing filter without affecting the built-in filters. The Filter Definition dialog box appears in every situation.

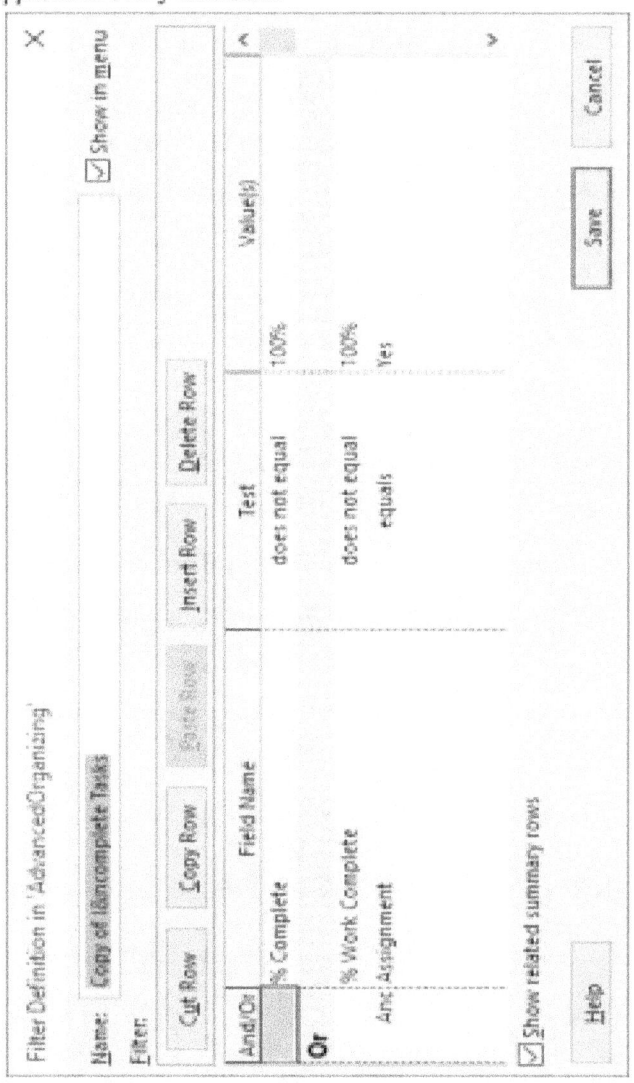

- Tasks that are not 100% complete (whether or not they have allocated resources) or tasks that are both less than 100% work complete and assigned to a resource will be displayed by the filter, which can be created using And/Or criteria.
- Name the filter if you selected New or Copy.
- Type in the desired filter criteria. Choose the Show related summary rows check box if you would want the resulting filter to show the summary rows of the tasks that the filter will display.
- Select "Save."

HOW TO APPLY A CUSTOM OR BUILT-IN FILTER TO ACTIVITIES OR RESOURCES

- Show the view that you wish to filter. To filter tasks, you must be in a task-centric view; to filter resources, you must be in a resource-centric view. The desired filter criterion does not have to be visible in the view.
- Click the Filter arrow in the Data group on the View tab (the box initially says [No Filter]).

Next, take one of the following actions:

- Select the desired filter criterion by clicking on it.

- Click More Filters, choose the desired filter, and then click Apply to filter the view if the desired filter criterion is not provided.

USING PRE-INSTALLED OR CUSTOM HIGHLIGHT FILTERS TO DRAW ATTENTION TO TASKS OR RESOURCES

Regular filters and highlight filters are comparable. Highlight filters apply a yellow highlight to details that fit the filter requirements rather than hiding those that don't.

- Show the view you wish to draw attention to.
- Click the Highlight arrow in the Data group on the View tab (the box initially says [No Highlight]).

Next, take one of the following actions

- Select the desired highlight criterion by clicking on it.
- To highlight the view, click More Highlights, choose the desired highlight filter, and then click Highlight if the desired highlight filter criterion is not displayed.

HOW TO REMOVE THE RESOURCES' OR TASKS' FILTERING OR HIGHLIGHTING

Take one of the following actions:

- Click the Filter arrow in the Data group on the View tab, and then select Clear Filter.
- Click the Highlight arrow in the Data group on the View tab, and then select Clear Highlight.
- In the column where you have filtered tasks or resources, click the AutoFilter arrow to the right of the column heading. To disable it, click Clear Filter.

MAKE NEW TABLES

You've worked with tables a lot by now. A table is a presentation of project data that resembles a spreadsheet and is arranged with horizontal rows and vertical columns. Each row denotes a single task or resource (or, in usage views, an assignment), while each column represents one of Project's several fields. If you are familiar with spreadsheets, the intersection of a column and a row is referred to as a cell; if you are more database-oriented, it is termed a field.

The Entry table in the Task Sheet view is an excellent illustration of a table. Every table in Project is tailored to display certain data. A number of tables that can be used in views are included in the project. Some of these tables, like the Entry and Summary tables, have already been shown to you. The fields you desire will probably be found in Project's built-in tables most of the time. Any built-in table, however, can be altered, or you can make a new table with only the information you require.

You might not need to make a new table if all you need to do is add a column to the existing one. In a table, you can simply add or remove columns (see to the procedures at the end of this chapter for information).

HOW TO MODIFY OR MAKE A UNIQUE TABLE

- Select Tables under the Data group on the View tab. Then, select More Tables to bring up the More Tables dialog box.

You can view every task and resource table that is available in the More Tables dialog box.

- To see that collection of tables, click Task or Resource.

Take one of these actions:

- To start from scratch and create a new table, click New.
- To make changes to an existing table, select it and click Edit.
- To create a new table based on an existing table, select it and then click Copy.

The Table Definition dialog box appears in every situation.

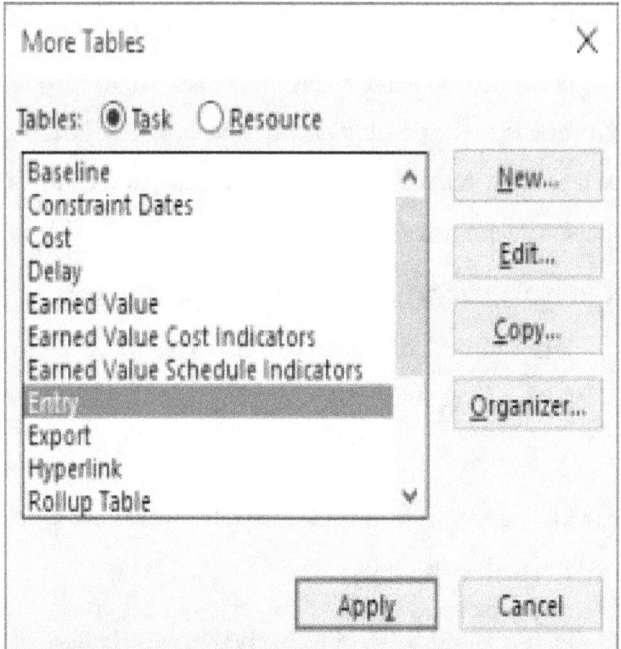

To rearrange or modify the fields in a table, use the Cut Row button and the other buttons (the fields are listed as rows in the dialog box, but they are columns in the table).

- Change or input the desired table definition values.
- To exit the Table Definition dialog box, click OK.

The name of your custom table appears under the Custom heading in the Tables list on the View tab if you checked the Show In Menu check box.

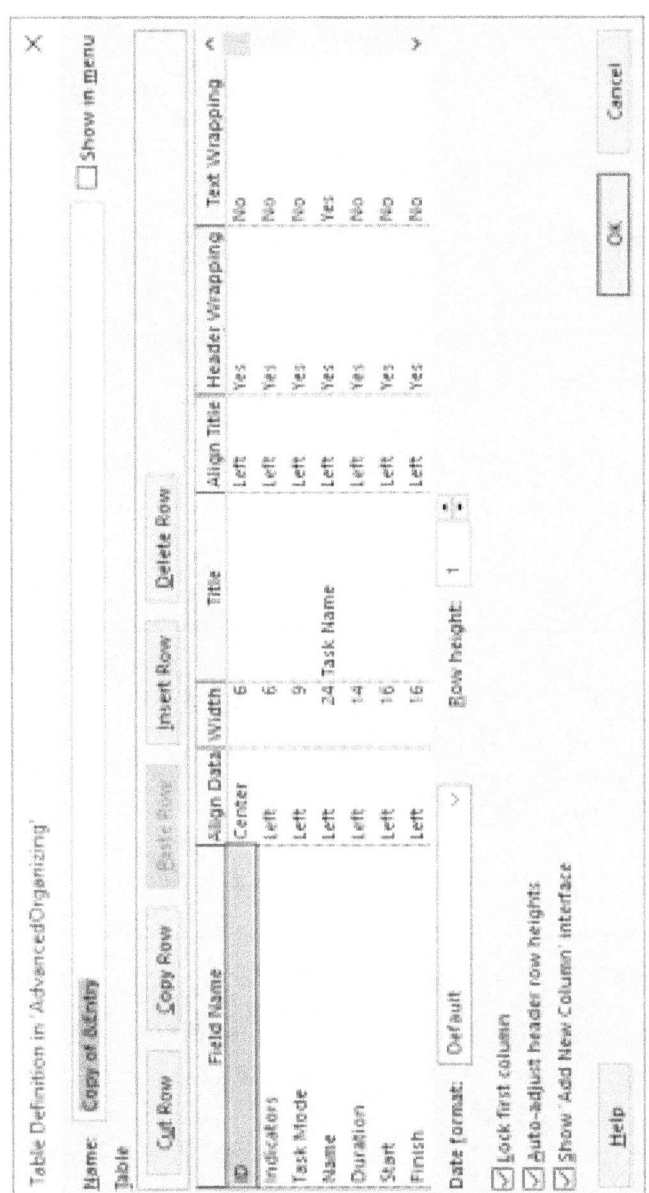

HOW TO MAKE A TABLE HAVE A COLUMN

- Decide which column you wish to add a new column to. When the new column is inserted, the selected column will be shifted to the right.
- Click Insert Column under the Columns group on the Format tab. Project shows every field that is available for the task or resource table type that you have selected.

By right-clicking on a column heading and choosing Insert Column from the shortcut menu, you may also add a new column to a table.

- Decide whatever field (column) you wish to include.

To delete a column, select Hide Column after performing a right-click on the column heading.

MAKE FRESH VIEWS

Almost everything you do in Project takes place in a vista. Elements like tables, groups, and filters may be included in a view. These can be used with visual components (like the task graphic in the chart section of a Gantt chart view) or other elements (like a timescaled grid in a usage view).

Dozens of perspectives are included in the project to arrange data for particular objectives. All of these views are displayed in the More Views dialog box.

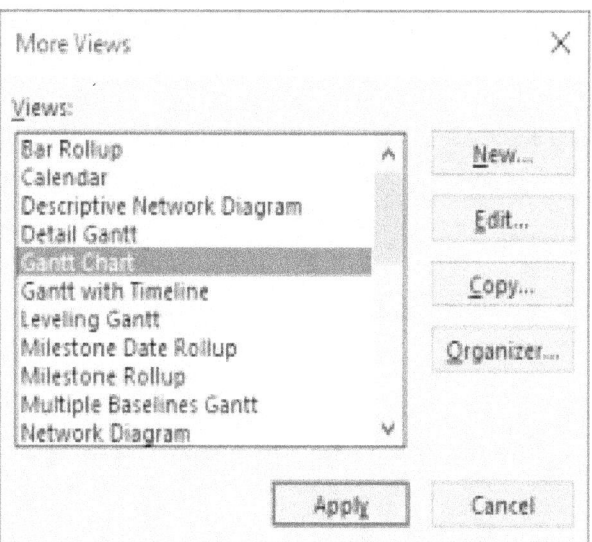

All of Project's views are listed in the More Views dialog box; you can modify or add your own views.

You may need to view the information in your plan in a different way than what the built-in views can provide. You can modify an existing view or make your own view if none of the views in Project suit your needs.

You can choose between a single-pane and multi-pane view for your new view. Although a view might have two distinct panes, most views only take up one pane. Actually, Project's default display consists of two panes: the Timeline and the Gantt Chart. You choose whether a new view will be task-centric or resource-centric when you build it. You then work in the View Definition dialog box in either scenario.

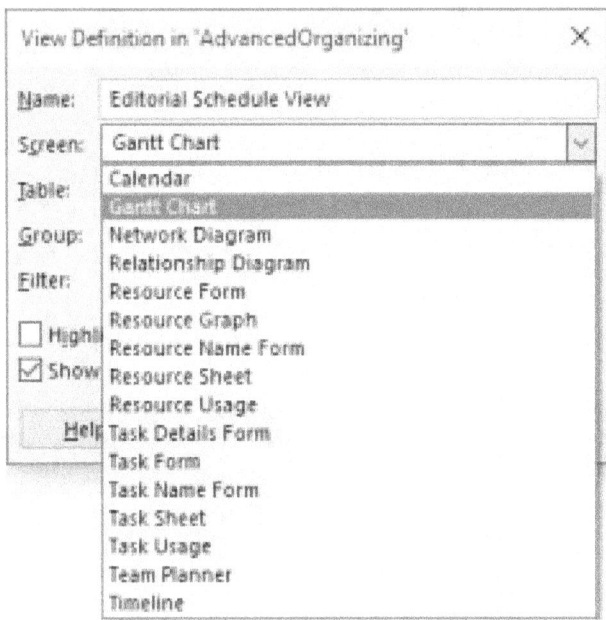

Every view is either resource-centric or task-centric. The type of view you chose in the Screen field determines which particular tables, groups, and filters are listed in the View Definition dialog box lists. For instance, only task-specific filters, such the Critical filter, are accessible in the Filter field if Task Sheet is selected in the Screen field. Additionally, different view types have different items available. For instance, the Table and Group choices are not available if you choose the Calendar view type.

Everywhere views are mentioned, new views show up under the Custom label for easy access.

HOW TO MAKE OR MODIFY A VIEW

- First, select Other Views from the Task Views or Resource Views group on the View tab. Next, select More Views to bring up the More Views dialog box. You can see every view that is accessible to you in this dialog box.

Take one of these actions:

- To start from scratch with a new view, click New. Next, choose one of the following actions in the Define New View dialog box:

Then select Single View.

- Press the Combination View button.

The two single-pane views (custom or built-in) that you want to utilize in the Combination view are specified when you choose Combination view. You finish defining the new view and go back to the More Views dialog box since the two single-pane views are already existing views.

- To make changes to an existing view, select it and click Edit.
- To build a new view based on an existing view, select it and then click Copy.

ADVICE

You can clone an existing view and make changes to the copy while maintaining the built-in views.

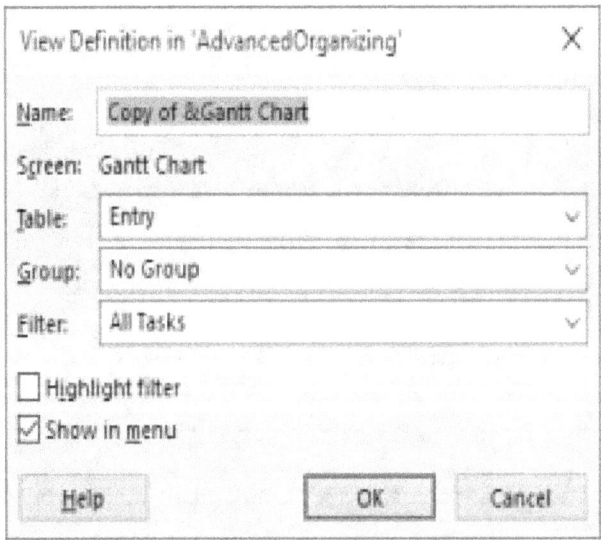

- The View Definition dialog box appears in every situation.

- None of the View Definition fields can be left empty when establishing a new view.

Choose or modify the desired view definition options:

- Use the ampersand and before a letter in the new view's name to set a keyboard shortcut for it.
- You can see every view type that Project supports in the Screen box. A table (like the Resource Sheet), a table and chart (like the Gantt Chart), or a form (like the Task Form) make up a lot of these views. Some views, like the Timeline and Network Diagram views, are only diagrammatic. Only when creating a new view is it possible to alter the screen type.
- Choose the default table that the view will include in the Table box. A single-pane view requires a table.
- You can add a custom or pre-existing group to your view definition in the Group box. Choose No Group if you do not wish to include a group.
- A built-in or custom filter can be included in the Filter box as part of your view definition. Choose All Tasks if you do not wish to apply a filter.

Alternatively, click the Highlight filter check box if you want the filter to highlight values without hiding them. The Show in Menu check box can be selected or cleared.

- To exit the View Definition dialog box, click OK.

ADVICE

The name of the view displays under the Custom heading in the related view type list on the View tab if you created a new view and checked the Show In Menu check box. A custom Gantt chart view, for instance, will show up in the Gantt Chart view list on the View tab.

DETAILS OF THE FILTER PLAN

The situation: Due to the resource-intensive nature of editing-related chores, you often have to look them up. Using a custom AutoFilter, you can rapidly display tasks linked to editing. Proceed with the following actions in the OrganizeDetails plan:

- Apply a custom AutoFilter to the Task Name column in the Gantt Chart view. Name contains edit is the filter's requirement.

To filter tasks that contain a particular term—in this case, "edit"—use a custom AutoFilter. Apply the custom AutoFilter, but do not save it. Your task list should only contain tasks with the label "edit" and their summary tasks 3 after using the customized AutoFilter. The custom AutoFilter should be removed from view.

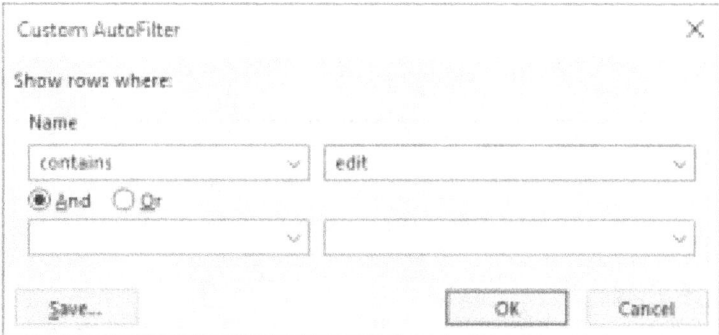

MAKE NEW TABLES

The situation: You keep working on the editorial duties for the new children's book plan. In order to achieve this, you choose to make a custom table and include some of the editorial task descriptions that have been added to a text field in the plan.

However, you will make one short-term modification to your Project settings before you build a new table. This change will keep this new table from appearing in other plans you may work with that have nothing to do with this training content. Proceed with the following actions in the OrganizeDetails plan:

- To access the Project Options dialog box, click the File tab and then select Options.

- After selecting Advanced, make sure the Automatically add new views, tables, filters, and groups to the global check box is checked under Display.
- To exit the Project Options dialog box, click OK. Now that you've finished the practice task's housekeeping, you may start making a new table.
- Make a duplicate of the Entry table in a new table.
- Give the newly created table the name Editorial Table and configure it to show up in the menu.
- Include the Editorial Focus (Text9) custom field in the table. Set its width to 20.

MAKE NEW VIEWS

The situation: You have effectively utilized the personalized table you previously designed to assist you in concentrating on editorial duties for the new children's book plan. This customization should now be combined into a unique view that you can quickly switch to at any time.

You will then return your Project option setting to its initial configuration in order to complete the practice tasks. Proceed with the following actions in the OrganizeDetails plan:

- Make a duplicate of the Gantt Chart view in a new view.
- Give the new view a name. Editing is in ongoing.
- Include the custom Editorial Table in the newly created view.
- In the new view, apply the Incomplete Tasks filter.
- Don't apply the new view to a group.

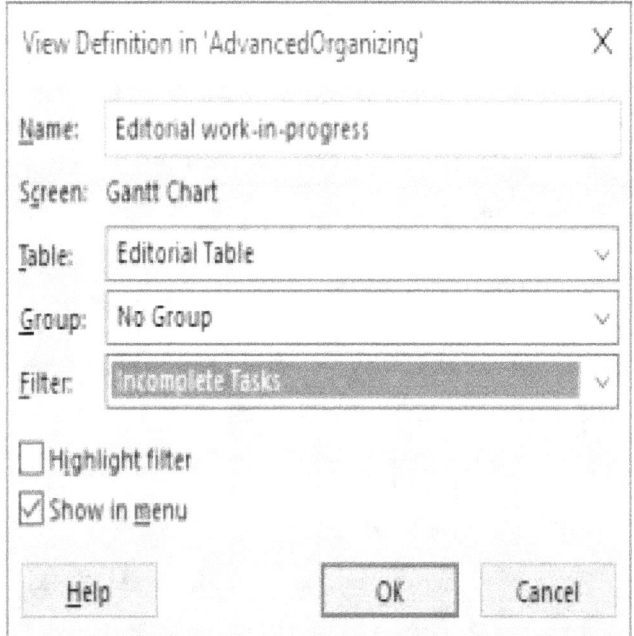

- Show the new view and include the custom table you previously built in the new custom view.

This is how your custom view ought to appear (notice the name of the custom view at the program window's left edge). The new custom view isn't available in other plans because of the housekeeping modification you made in the last set of practice activities. You will likely want your custom views to be accessible in any plan when you develop them, so you will return the display setting to its default configuration. In this manner, any future custom views you develop will be accessible in any plan you use.

- To access the Project Options dialog box, click the File tab and then select Options.
- Select the Automatically add new views, tables, filters, and groups to the global check box under Display after clicking Advanced.
- To exit the Project Options dialog box, click OK.

HOW TO DOCUMENT THE AMOUNT OF WORK COMPLETED AND LEFT ON EACH TASK

- To open the Task Usage view, select Task Usage under the Task Views group on the View tab.
- To view the Work table, select Tables under the Data group on the View tab, and then select Work.
- Enter an actual work value in the Actual column for the task for which you wish to record actual work.

- You can change the task's Remaining Work value if you'd like.

HOW TO DOCUMENT COMPLETED AND UNFINISHED WORK FOR EACH ASSIGNMENT

- Show the Work table and the Task Usage view.
- Enter an actual work value in the Actual column for the designated resource for which you wish to record actual work.
- You can change the assignment's Remaining Work value if you'd like.

Keep track of the time-phased actual work for projects and tasks. This article presents methods for tracking work over time, such as real work accomplished daily or weekly. Tracking work by time period is sometimes referred to as tracking timephased actuals since information dispersed throughout time is sometimes described as being timephased. This is the most thorough level of progress tracking that Project offers.

Similar to the more straightforward tracking techniques, monitoring time-phased actuals enables you to answer the most fundamental project management queries:

Are things beginning and ending on schedule? If not, how will this affect the project's completion date?

Are resources taking longer or shorter than anticipated to do tasks? Is the cost of completing activities more or lower than anticipated?

If resources must notify the project management of their daily or weekly actuals, entering time-phased actuals necessitates more work from them as well as more effort from the project manager. Nevertheless, compared to other techniques of tracking progress, time-phased actuals provide you with a great deal more information about the task and resource status of the plan. If your strategy or set of tasks contains the following, entering time-phased values may be the best course of action:

High-risk assignments tasks with a limited turnaround time, for which even a one-day deviation could jeopardize the project as a whole Tasks for which you want to create or verify throughput metrics, or the rates at which a given amount of a deliverable can be finished in a given amount of time. Activities in which sponsors or other interested parties are particularly interested Activities that call for labor to be billed on an hourly basis. Use the Task Usage or Resource

Usage view's Work table and timephased grid to track actual work at the most detailed level imaginable.

You can insert time-phased actual work at the task or assignment level in the Task Usage view. Actuals are entered at the assignment level in the Resource Usage view. In both views, Project will update the work values spread over time in the right half of the view when actual work is entered on the left side. In this topic, we'll examine the opposite: entering real work in the view's time-phased side and viewing the outcomes for each task or assignment on the left side.

The Task Usage view was used in the example in the previous article; we'll start with the Resource Usage view in this one. Assignments for each resource are displayed in the Resource Usage view.

ADVICE

In a use view, you can modify the information (i.e., the fields) displayed in the time-phased grid. Fields can be added or removed, and the displayed fields' formatting can be altered. You can include the Actual Work field, for instance. Click Add Details in the Details group on the Format tab to view the fields and formatting options that are available. Actual work values for individual tasks can be entered in both views on a daily, weekly, or any other time period you choose (by modifying the timeline). For instance, you can input three distinct values on a time-phased grid if a task has three resources assigned to it and you know that two of the resources worked on the assignment for eight hours one day and the third resource worked for six hours.

Correctly establishing the timescale is essential to working efficiently in a use view. To manage the time period in which you enter actual values in the time-phased grid, you can adjust the timescale's zoom level. You can, for instance, alter the timeline to display weeks instead of days; if you enter a number at the weekly level, it is dispersed across the week.

The project features a number of useful shortcuts for navigating through the usage views' time-phased grid side. The earliest scheduled work on the chosen task or assignment can be seen in the Task Usage view by using the Scroll To Task button on the Task Tab, in the Editing group. In the task shortcut menu, you can also use the Scroll To Task command. To examine the scheduled work for the selected resource or assignment, utilize the Scroll To Task option in the Resource Usage view. Using the Go To command via the keyboard shortcut Ctrl+G, you can rapidly navigate to a particular date in the grid (or a task or resource ID) in both views. Simply type "go to" into the Tell Me box, and Project will display the command if you can't remember it.

This is an illustration of how to enter time-phased actuals in a usage view. The scheduled work for each task, resource, or assignment is equal on both sides of a usage view, as you saw in the last article. The scheduled work is distributed throughout time on the right side, while it is displayed as a single total value on the left.

The real work completed on the task is allocated to its assignments, as you saw in the previous topic. The time-phased grid shows the distribution of real work by time period.

To access the Backstage view, select the File tab and then select Options. Choose the desired default time increment in the Work Is Entered In box on the Schedule page of the Project Options dialog box. The assignment's actual work will next be entered into the time-phased grid.

The project modified the planned work to take into consideration the recorded actual work values that deviated from the planned work. Project records the real work to match the scheduled work in the time-phased grid on the right side of the use view when you enter actual work in the table on the left side of the view. The ability to carefully regulate the dates for which the actual work is recorded is the primary benefit of entering actual work in the timephased grid rather than the table on the left side of the display.

CHAPTER NINE
FOCUS OF PROJECT MANAGEMENT: GATHER DATA FROM RESOURCES

A timecard and the Resource Usage view are comparable. In fact, you may need a paper timecard or its electronic counterpart in order to record assignment-level actual work values. Assuming that you need to track actual and remaining work at this level of detail, there are a number of ways to gather this data from resources. Among the collection techniques are the following:

Gather real values on your own. If you only interact with a limited number of resources frequently—for example, once a week during a status meeting—this approach is doable. Additionally, it's an excellent chance to speak with the resources directly about any obstacles they may be facing or any surprises (positive or negative) they may have had while working on the project.

Utilize a formal status reporting mechanism to get actuals. This method may be able to accommodate your organization's current hierarchy and accomplish more than just reporting project status.

Be mindful that resources may be concerned about how their real work values represent their overall performance.

regardless of the data collection techniques you employ. Although schedule actuals may be helpful in project management, performance evaluation is more of a business management issue than a project management one.

You may be able to use this timecard data in Project as time-phased actuals if your company has a timecard reporting system. Although you might not need to track at this level, you can use the data and save yourself some effort if resources fill out timesheets for other reasons (such as paying other departments within the company).

Speaking of timecards, you may want to look into Project Professional and its compatibility with Microsoft SharePoint and Project Web App (PWA), depending on how your company runs.

The values of tasks and assignments are closely linked; changes to one have an immediate impact on the other. But if you want to, you can end this connection. By doing this, you can manually enter the actual numbers for the tasks to which those resources are assigned and track progress for resource assignments, for instance. Generally speaking, you shouldn't sever this relationship unless your company has unique reporting requirements, such as when you have to adhere to a status reporting methodology that is based on something other than the actual numbers entered for assignments in plans. Do the following to end this relationship: To access the Backstage view, select the File tab and then select Options. Clear the Updating Task Status Updates Resource Status check box under the Calculation Options For This Project label on the Schedule tab of the Project Options dialog box. You cannot apply this setting to just certain tasks inside a plan; it applies to the entire plan that is now open.

USING THE TASK USAGE VIEW TO DOCUMENT TIME-PHASED ACTUAL WORK

- To open the Task Usage view, select Task Usage under the Task Views group on the View tab.
- Select Actual Work from the Details group on the Task Usage Tools Format tab. The time-phased section of the view displays the Actual Work detail row.

If necessary, modify the timeline to correspond with the period of time you wish to start working on actual tasks (daily or weekly, for instance):

- Click the timeframe arrow in the Zoom group on the View tab, and then select the desired timeframe time unit.

- Enter an actual work value in the time-phased grid at the point where the task or assignment and the desired date intersect.

HOW TO DOCUMENT ACTUAL LABOR THAT IS TIME-PHASED IN THE RESOURCE USAGE VIEW

- Show the Actual Work detail and Resource Usage view, and modify the timeline as necessary.
- Enter an actual work value in the time-phased grid where an assignment and the desired date intersect.

RESCHEDULED UNFINISHED WORK

Sometimes during a project, work may be halted for a particular task or for the duration of the project. Project can reschedule the remaining tasks to begin after the date you designate if this occurs.

When you reschedule unfinished work, you designate the new date as the one on which work can start again. The Update Project dialog box allows you to reschedule unfinished work.

Regarding the rescheduled date, Project manages tasks as follows:

The entire task is rescheduled to start after the rescheduled date if there is no actual work recorded for it before then and no constraint is applied.

The assignment is divided so that all remaining work begins after the rescheduled date if there is some real work recorded before the rescheduled date but none later. There is no impact on the real task. The assignment remains unaffected if there is some real work assigned to it both before and after the postponed date.

HOW TO POSTPONE UNFINISHED TASKS

- Choose the individual tasks you want to reschedule first.
- To access the Update Project dialog box, click Update Project in the Status group on the Project tab.
- Choose Reschedule unfinished work to begin after, then type or choose the desired date in the date box.

Take one of these actions:

- To reschedule work just for the chosen tasks, click Selected Tasks.
- To reschedule work for the entire project, click Entire Project.
- Press OK.

HOW TO OPEN THE PROJECT STATISTICS DIALOG BOX

To bring up the dialog box for Project Statistics:

- To access the Backstage view, click the File tab. Next, select the Info tab.

- Click Project Information on the Backstage view's Info page, and then click
- Project Data.

To show a dashboard report, which includes reports on project overview, cost overview, and burndown

- Select Dashboards under the View Reports group on the Report tab.
- Select the desired Dashboard report by clicking.

HOW TO DETERMINE WHICH TASKS HAVE FALLEN BEHIND

Schedule variance occurs when duties begin or end earlier or later than anticipated. Delays in beginning or completing tasks are one reason for schedule deviation. Tasks that started late or those that might start later than expected are definitely things you want to know about. Let's examine several methods for identifying task variance.

One useful approach for seeing task variance graphically is the Tracking Gantt view. The distinction between scheduled, actual, and baseline performance is visually shown in this image. The tasks on the critical path are indicated by color in the Tracking Gantt view. This is particularly crucial when examining variance since it has a direct impact on the plan's completion date for vital tasks. You may determine whether tasks have deviated from their initial baseline schedule by comparing the Gantt bars that are currently scheduled with the baseline Gantt bars.

Point to any bar or other item in a Gantt chart view to view more information about it. A ScreenTip containing information shows after a brief pause. For determining deviation from the baseline, the Task Sheet's Variance table or any other task-centric tabular representation is particularly helpful. The number of days of variance for each task's start and finish dates is displayed in the variance table.

ADVICE

You can use the Slipping Tasks filter to narrow down the task list to only include tasks with variance. Only unfinished tasks that have deviated from their baseline schedule since they were last scheduled are displayed by this filter. "Slipping" in this sense refers to "slipping from baseline." The Late Tasks and Slipped/Late Progress filters are additional helpful filters.

The Slipping Tasks and Late Tasks reports are two helpful reports that address task variance. Unless you specify a different status date, the current date is the main emphasis of the Late Tasks report. To concentrate on work that have completed or will end later than anticipated, use the Late work report. Task status in respect to the tasks' baseline completion dates is the main emphasis of the Slipping Tasks report. The Slipping Tasks report assists you in determining which tasks have deviated from the baseline when a plan has one.

TO SHOW THE VARIANCE TABLE IN THE VIEW OF THE TASK SHEET

The Variance table can also be included in any task-focused tabular view.

- To see the Task Sheet view, select Other Views under the Task Views group on the View tab. Then, select Task Sheet.
- Select Tables under the Data group on the View menu, and then select Variance.

HOW TO SHOW THE GANTT CHART FOR TRACKING

- Click the Gantt Chart arrow on the Task Views group on the View tab, and then select Tracking Gantt.

HOW TO SHOW THE REPORT ON LATE OR SLIPPING TASKS

- Click In Progress under the View Reports group on the Report tab.
- Select the desired report by clicking.

ANALYZE THE COSTS OF THE TASK

Although it is essential to almost all projects, monitoring the status of the schedule—that is, identifying which tasks begin and end on time—is only one way to assess the general health of the project. Cost variation is another crucial metric for projects with cost data: are tasks exceeding or falling short of budget?

The following are examples of task expenses in a project: Tasks with fixed costs applied directly Assignment-derived resource costs, Cost variance occurs when tasks cost more or less to perform than anticipated. You may prevent going over your overall budget by making small budget modifications for individual tasks by evaluating cost variation.

Despite the clear relationship between activities and resources (and their costs), it is instructive to assess each one separately. The views, reports, and other tools that assist you in determining and communicating task costs are the main emphasis of this topic. The same is true for resource costs in the next topic.

Displaying the Cost table in any task-centric tabular view, like the Task Sheet, is an excellent place to start. To view the entire cost rollup from subtasks to summary tasks to the project summary task, display the project summary task.

The total cost of a task is shown in this table as the cost of the assigned resources and their assignment durations, plus any fixed costs that have been defined for the work. This cost is frequently referred to as the scheduled cost. Total Cost equals the task's real cost if the task has been finished. When analyzing the expenditures of a plan, it is helpful to display the project summary task (designated as task 0).

The cost figures shown in the Project Statistics dialog box correspond to the plan's cost values for the project summary task. Among these values are the following:

- The sum of the actual (completed) and remaining (unfinished) cost values is the current total cost value.
- The project's anticipated cost at the time the baseline was established is known as the baseline cost value. The cost that has been incurred thus far is the actual cost.

The difference between the present and real costs is the residual cost.

Task costs are the subject of multiple reports throughout the project. Numerous tables and charts in the Task Cost Overview report provide both summary and in-depth task cost data.

Task expenses are totaled by their completion status in the Task Cost Overview report's Cost Distribution pie graphic.

The Cash Flow report is another helpful tool. This report displays the total project costs for each quarter, or for whatever time period you choose for budgeting.

HOW TO VIEW THE PLAN'S COST AND CUMULATIVE COST VALUES OVER TIME, DISPLAY THE CASH FLOW REPORT

A graphic report will conclude our tour of the task-centric and cost-centric project elements. Project data that has been exported to Excel or Visio is used in visual reports. The budget (in this case, as currently scheduled), baseline, and actual expenses for each time period are displayed in the Budget Cost visual report. Project creates a PivotTable, exports data to Excel, and then generates the chart in Excel when you make this visual report. Based on an Excel PivotTable, the Budget Cost visual report provides the extensive data manipulation capabilities of a PivotTable.

Here are some more pointers and recommendations for handling task cost data:

- Use the assigned late/overbudget tasks, to search for a particular resource. This filter is accessible through the Filters command in the Data group and the More Filters list on the View tab.
- By selecting Work from the Tables menu accessible from the View tab, in the Data group, you may display the work variance in the Work table in a task view. Keep in mind that analyzing work variance is one method of analyzing cost variance for a plan where the majority of expenses are produced from work resources.

In a use view, time-phased baseline and scheduled work can be compared. For instance, pick Baseline Work in the Details group on the Format tab in the Task Usage view.

Navigate to the Task Usage view and use the Cost table to see the cost variance over time for task assignments. The Add Details dialog box allows you to display Cost, Baseline Cost, and Actual Cost details when in a use view. Choose the desired options from the Details group on the Format tab.

to show the Task Sheet view 1's Cost table. Click Other Views under the Task Views group on the View tab, and then select Task sheet to bring up the view of the Task Sheet.

- Select Tables under the Data group on the View menu, and then select Cost.

HOW TO SHOW THE CASH FLOW REPORT OR TASK COST OVERVIEW

- Select Costs from the View Reports group on the Report tab.
- Select the desired report by clicking.

The Budget Cost visual report must be displayed using Excel.

- To launch the Visual Reports dialog box, select Visual Reports under the Export group on the Report tab.
- Select the tab for Assignment Usage.
- After selecting Budget Cost Report, select View. Excel is used to display the report.3

ANALYZE THE COSTS OF RESOURCES

As a way to gauge project progress and variance, project managers occasionally concentrate on resource costs. Information on resource costs, however, also meets the needs of other people. Monitoring resource costs closely may have a direct impact on an organization's financial health because for many, they are the main, if not the only, expenses incurred during project completion. The person most interested in resource costs on projects in relation to organizational costs may not be a project manager but rather an executive, cost accountant, or resource manager.

Billing, either internally (for instance, by charging another department for services your department has rendered) or externally, is another frequent justification for monitoring resource costs. In either scenario, the resource cost data that is kept in plans can be used as the foundation for billing other people for the services that your department or organization provides.

This topic explains how to focus on resource costs in your plans using some useful features, views, and reports. We start with the Cost table, which can be shown in any tabular view that is focused on resources, like the Resource Sheet view.

Each resource's cost rate is multiplied by the amount of work they do on the tasks they are assigned to in the plan to determine the cost values for work resources.

The cost, baseline cost, and associated cost values for each resource are displayed in the Cost table.

You can then sort the Cost or another column from largest to smallest while the Cost table is visible. The values in the Cost column, which are the total of the resources' actual (or historical) and remaining (or anticipated) costs, are used by Project to sort resources. You can quickly determine which resources are the most and least expensive overall by sorting them by the Cost column.

Sorting resources according to their variance value is another practical sorting method. You can easily identify the resources with the biggest variance by sorting the resource list by cost variance. Use the sorting and filtering capabilities to arrange and present resource cost information in tabular views

To observe cost variance over time for assignments per resource, display the Resource Usage view, and then apply the Cost table. Then you may additionally show Cost and Baseline Cost data in the timephased grid. This also works in the Task Usage view.

With both the Cost table and cost-related timephased details exposed, the Resource Usage view gives you a detailed level of timephased cost data. Project also offers studies that focus on resource costs, such as the Resource Cost Overview report.

The Resource Cost Overview report offers a mix of charts and tables that focus on cost specifics per resource. This report offers a basic summary table of resource cost statistics, including graphics that represent actual and remaining costs per resource, and cost totals by resource type. The Cost Distribution pie chart is especially crucial if your strategy contains a considerable portion of material and cost resources.

HOW TO DISPLAY THE COST TABLE IN THE RESOURCE SHEET VIEW

- To open the Resource Sheet view, select Resource Sheet within the Resource Views group on the View tab.
- Select Tables under the Data group on the View menu, and then select Cost.

HOW TO SORT RESOURCES BY COST AMOUNTS

- Display the Cost table.

- Click the AutoFilter arrow in a column heading such as Cost or Variance, and in the option that opens, click Sort Largest to Smallest.

HOW TO DISPLAY THE COST TABLE AND COST INFORMATION IN THE RESOURCE USAGE VIEW

- On the View tab, under the Resource Views group, click Resource Usage to display the Resource Usage view.
- Select Tables under the Data group on the View menu, and then select Cost. The Cost table appears in the Resource Usage view.
- To add the Cost detail to the time-phased side of the view, select it from the Details group on the Resource Usage Tools Format tab.
- Click Add features to access the Detail Styles dialog box and add more time-phased features. Next, select the cost-related fields you wish to add from the list of Available Fields, and then select Show.

The Resource Cost Overview report will be displayed.

- Select Costs from the View Reports group on the Report tab.
- Select Overview of Resource Costs.

CHAPTER TEN

FORMAT AND PRINT VIEWS: COMPREHENSIVE METHODS

Project offers several formatting features that are comparable to those of a style-based word processor like Microsoft Word, where applying a style once changes all of the information in the document. Throughout a plan, you can alter the look of a certain kind of Gantt bar, like a summary bar, in Project by using styles. Additional formatting choices covered in this chapter concentrate on styling some of the more popular views and activities directly. Using Project's more extensive formatting and printing capabilities, this chapter walks you through the steps involved in formatting and printing views.

SET UP A GANTT CHART

Although just one view is explicitly named the Gantt Chart view, keep in mind that a number of built-in views are Gantt chart views. The Detail Gantt, Leveling Gantt, Multiple Baselines Gantt, and Tracking Gantt are additional Gantt chart views. A presentation that displays Gantt bars arranged on a timeline is commonly referred to as a "Gantt chart view."

In a Gantt chart view, you can format particular item categories to alter how that kind of item looks. The Bar Styles dialog box, which may be accessed from the Bar Grouping styles on the Format tab. Only that view of the Gantt chart will be affected by formatting changes you make to the bar style and other elements.

To alter the look of entire item categories in Gantt chart views, use the Bar Styles dialog box. Any formatting adjustments you make to a certain bar type (important tasks, for instance) or other element in this dialog box will affect all of that bars or items in the Gantt chart. In accordance with the sequence specified in the Bar Styles dialog box, Project displays bars and other items on a bar row. The potential for one bar to be stacked over (and obscure) another bar (or other feature) is thus introduced. For instance, Project places progress bars on top of task bars since the task bar style is higher in the Bar Styles list than the progress bar style. In most cases, you will receive the expected outcomes. Examine the Bar Styles dialog box's item order if you're not getting the desired results.

You can add or remove items, as well as alter the formatting of objects that can show up in a Gantt chart view (such the Gantt bar for a task). Comparing baseline, interim, and scheduled plans in one view, for instance, could be helpful. The Bar Styles dialog box already displays the baseline and scheduled Gantt bars, but interim Gantt Bars are not. Let's go through the process of adding them. In the Bar Styles dialog box, you would first add a new row. You should pay attention to the sequence of the Gantt bars since Project will draw them in the same order as they are stated in the Bar Styles dialog box.

You then input the desired information for the new Interim Gantt bar. For this example, you want Project to create interim Gantt charts for routine tasks, using the Start1 and Finish1 values from the interim plan as the From and To dates. For regular tasks, the new Gantt bar style called Interim will show up in this example. It will be on the second bar row and span the Start1 through Finish1 dates of the interim plan. As of right now, you have told Project to show the start and end dates of the first intermediate plan as bars. The lowest portion of the Bar Styles dialog box will then be your main focus. There, you will alter the new bar style's visual appeal.

Assume for the purposes of this example that you want the Gantt bars for your interim plan to be full-height and solid green.

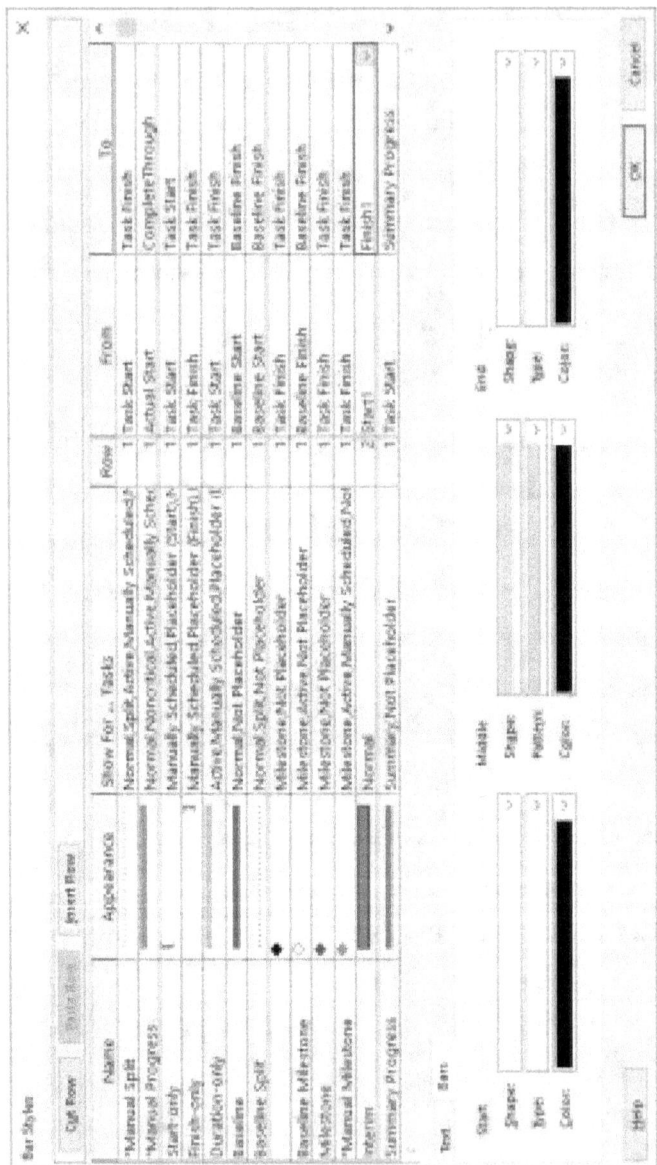

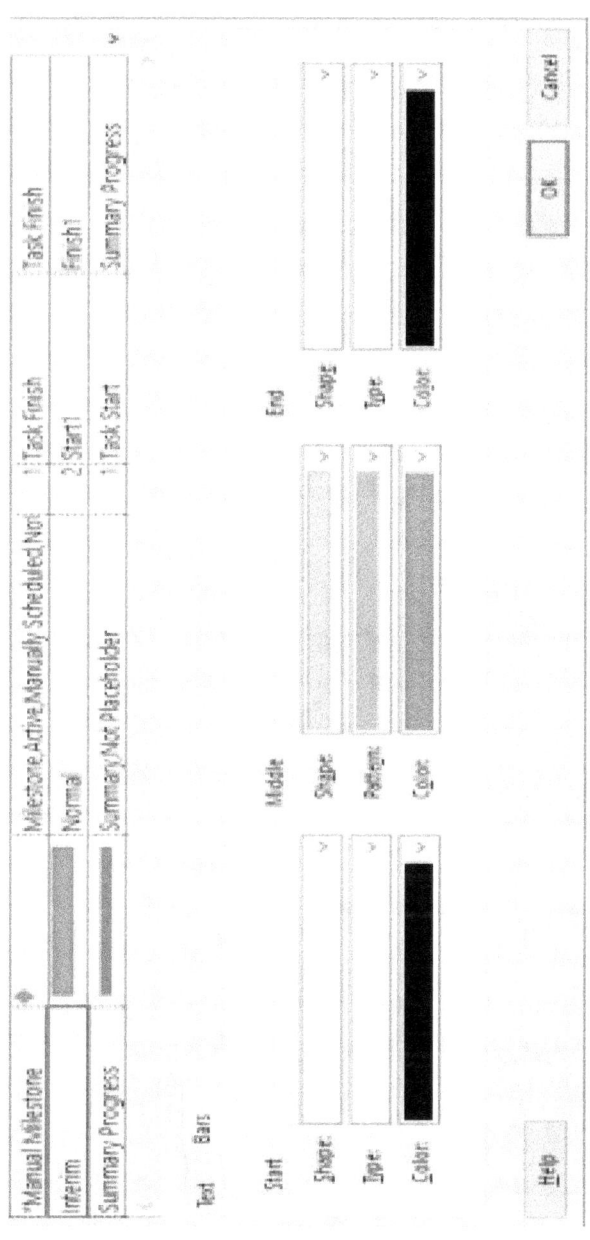

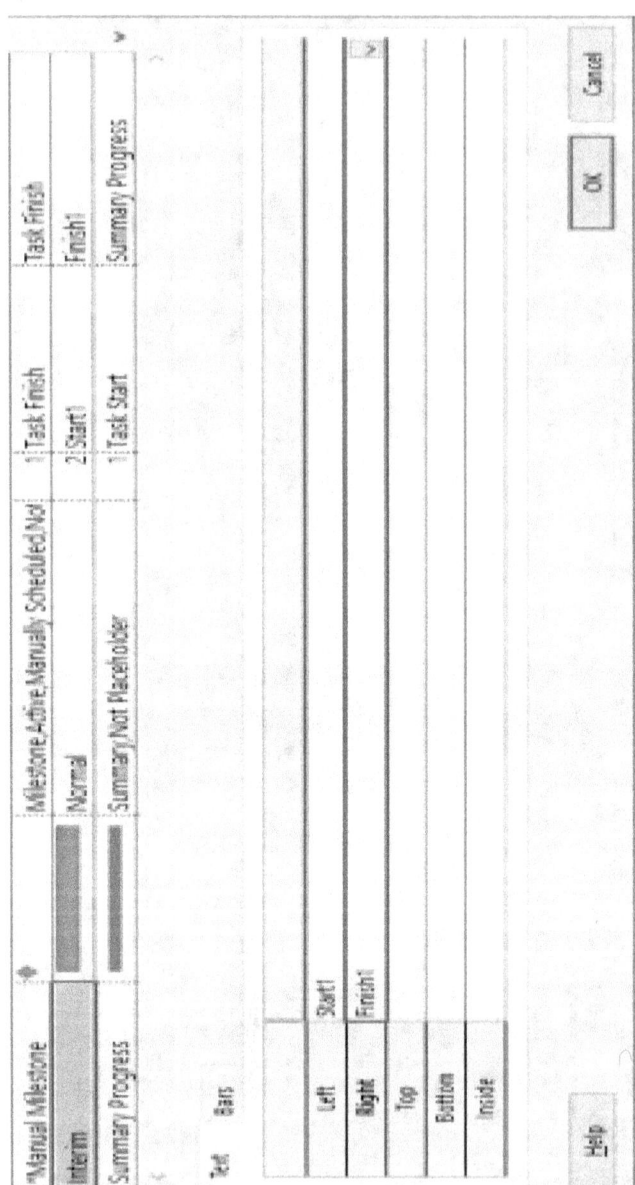

This illustration uses a solid green format for the new Interim Gantt bar layout. Setting the wording you want to appear in or around each interim Gantt bar will complete your custom Gantt bar definition. The intermediate bars for these Gantt bars should display the start and end dates that are entered in the Start1 and Finish1 fields on either side of the bar.

In addition to the features covered in this topic, Project provides a number of additional Gantt chart formatting features. Take a look at these buttons on the Format page to investigate further formatting options: Use the Format group's Text Styles button to format text related to a particular task type, like summary task text. The timeline labels, bar text, and summary task names can all be formatted using the Text Styles button. Use the Layout button in the Format group to format how Gantt bars and link lines look.

You may easily switch which baseline is displayed (for instance, on the Tracking Gantt Chart view) if you saved multiple baselines (Baseline and Baselines 1 through 10). The Baseline button in the Bar Styles category is how you accomplish this. In the Bar Styles dialog box, Project automatically changes the From and To values for the baseline bars and elements to match the values of the baseline you presented as you work. The Bar Styles dialog box will display the options you select in the Bar Styles group on the Format tab (except from the Format button itself).

HOW TO DESIGN A NEW GANTT CHART

- Change the view to a Gantt chart.
- To enter the Bar Styles dialog box, select Format in the Bar Styles group on the Gantt Chart Tools Format tab, and then click Bar Styles.

Double-clicking the chart portion's backdrop in a Gantt chart view or right-clicking the background and selecting Bar Styles from the shortcut menu are two other ways to bring up this dialog box.

- Choose the row to add the new Gantt bar style to in the Bar Styles dialog box. Keep in mind that Project displays Gantt charts according to the sequence specified in the Bar Styles dialog box. Fourth, select Insert Row. The project adds a row to the table for a new kind of bar.
- Type in the desired name for the updated bar style.

Keep in mind that if you begin the name of a bar style with an asterisk (*), you can stop it from showing up in a printed legend.

- You can choose the task type (regular, summary, or milestone) or task status (critical or in progress) that the bar will reflect in the Show For…Tasks area

By first choosing the task type in the Show For…Tasks field and then typing Not before the task type's name, you may create a bar style that excludes particular task kinds. In order to remove summary tasks from a bar style, for instance, you must first add Summary to the Show for…Tasks field and then change it to Not Summary. The built-in bar styles provide numerous examples of task type exclusions.

- Double-click in the Show For… Tasks section, then type the names of the extra task types you wish to add to the same bar style. Use a comma to separate the names of each task type. The built-in bar styles include several examples of various task types for each bar design.
- Choose the row in which the bar will show up in the Row field. Up to four bar rows are allowed for each task.

- Choose the bar's beginning and ending positions in the From and To fields. Enter the same Task Finish value in the From and To fields for milestone shapes.
- Select the Bars tab in the lower section of the Bar Styles dialog box.
- Select the desired bar style's Start, Middle, and End display settings. The Appearance column shows the display options you have chosen for the bar.
- Use the stages in the following procedure to add text values to the new bar style. Click OK if you do not wish to input text values at this time.

HOW TO ADD OR MODIFY TEXT THAT IS SHOWN USING A GANTT CHART

- Launch the dialog box for bar styles.
- Choose the desired bar style in the Bar Styles dialog box.
- Select the Text tab in the lower portion of the Bar Styles dialog box.
- Choose a field value in the row that matches the desired text location in relation to the bar.

You can frequently start typing the name of the item you wish to select from a list like this, and then select it when its complete name appears. For instance, Project displays the values that start with the letter when you type. The values that start with the letters displayed by Project if you write next.

- Click OK after adding any more text values you desire.

HOW TO CHANGE THE DRAWING PRECEDENCE ORDER, REARRANGE THE BAR STYLES

- Launch the dialog box for bar styles.
- In the drawing precedence order, choose the name of the bar style you want to move up or down.
- Select "Cut Row."
- Choose the row in which the first bar style is to be moved.
- After selecting Paste Row, select OK.

CREATE A TIMELINE VIEW

The Timeline view is a convenient method to see the "big picture" of the plan. One Timeline view can have one or more timeline bars displayed, and each timeline bar can be customized separately.

Jason Taylor

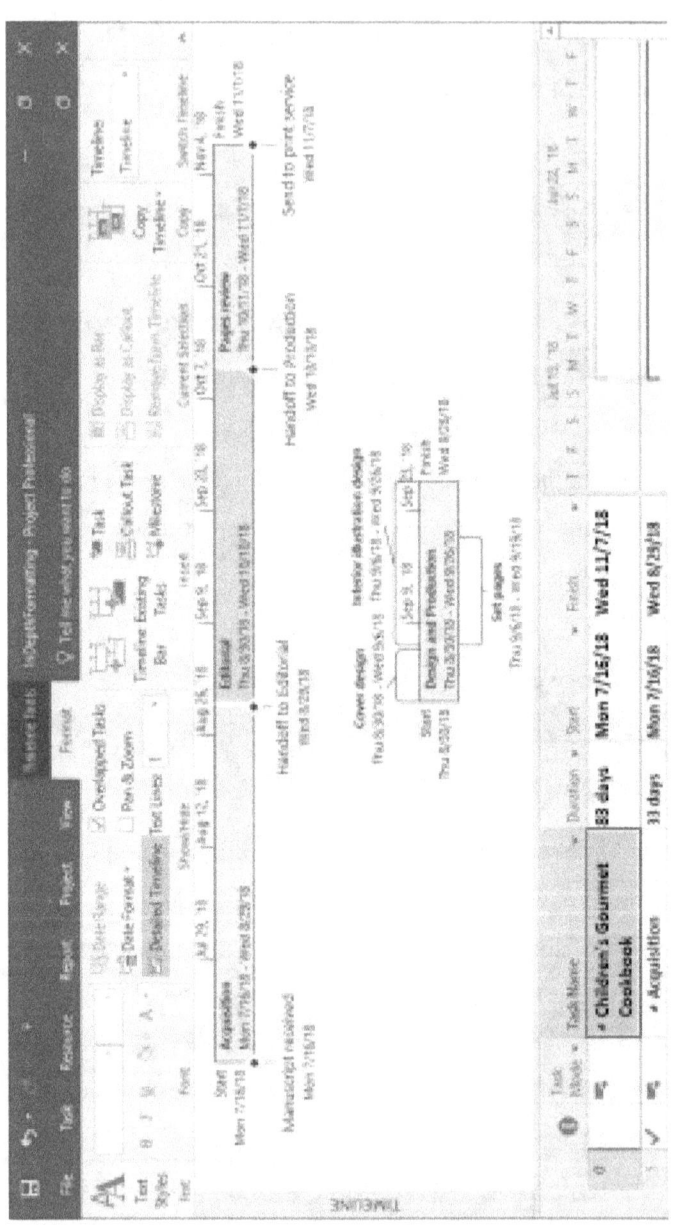

The Format tab's buttons alter when you place the emphasis in the Timeline view; keep in mind that the Format tab is contextual, meaning it adjusts according to what is selected at the moment. A timeline bar's default formatting may be sufficient for your purposes, but if not, you can alter its appearance. Text styles can be used to format the text of whole timeline item categories, such as all milestone dates.

You can format an item directly in a Timeline view, as well as reformat item categories using styles. Select the item and use the Format tab's buttons to achieve the desired outcome.

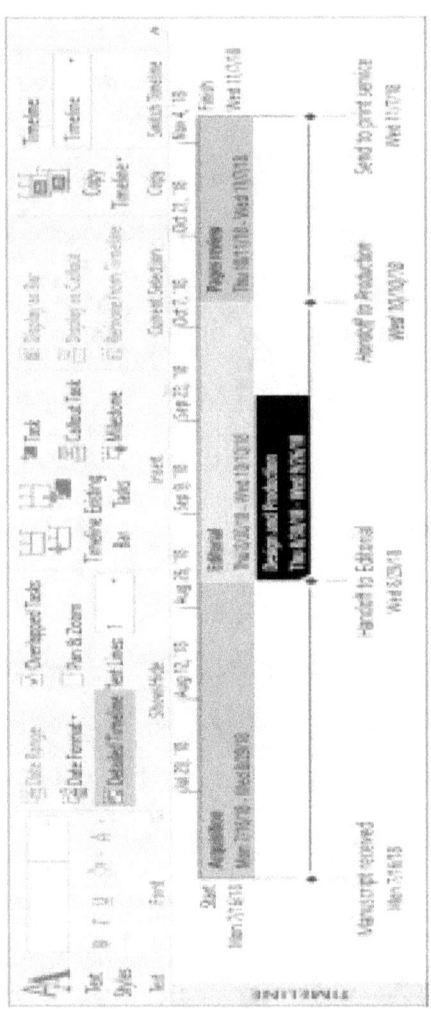

You can format each timeline separately when you add more than one timeline to a single Timeline view. This allows you a lot of freedom in using the Timeline view to highlight key components of your overall plan, including the last tasks in certain work phases. One excellent Project view for sharing with others via email, a paper, or a presentation is the Timeline view.

HOW TO ALTER THE TEXT STYLES OF THE TIMELINE

- To display the Timeline view, if required, check the Timeline check box in the Split View group on the View tab.
- Select the Timeline Tools Format tab after clicking anywhere in the Timeline view.
- To access the Text Styles dialog box, click Text Styles in the Text group on the Format tab.
- Choose the kind of timeline item whose style you wish to modify from the Item to Change list in the dialog box.
- Click OK after applying the desired formatting settings for the chosen item type.

HOW TO FORMAT AN ITEM IN A TIMELINE DIRECTLY

- Select the item you want to format in the Timeline view.
- Apply the desired formatting settings in the Font group on the Format tab.

Additionally, you can use the formatting choices on the Mini Toolbar that shows when you right-click on an item you wish to modify.

HOW TO EXPAND THE TIMELINE VIEW BY ADDING MORE TIMELINE BARS (UP TO 10)

- In the Timeline view, click anywhere.
- Click Timeline Bar in the Insert group on the Format tab. The Timeline view gains a new timeline bar from Project. At first, it is vacant.
- Click Existing tasks to enter the Add Tasks To Timeline dialog box on the Format tab, in the Insert group, after making sure the new timeline bar is selected.
- Select the tasks you wish to include in the new timeline bar in the dialog box, and then select OK.

The Timeline view allows you to drag and drop tasks between timeline bars. A timeline bar can be deleted by right-clicking on it and selecting Remove From Timeline.

HOW TO CHANGE THE RANGE OF DATES THAT A TIMELINE BAR IS SHOWN OVER

- First, select a timeline bar.

- To access the Set Timeline Dates dialog box, select Date Range under the Show/Hide group on the Format tab.
- Click OK after choosing your desired start and end dates in the dialog box.

CREATE A VIEW OF A NETWORK DIAGRAM

A network diagram is a common method used in conventional project management to show the relationships between project activities. The relationships between tasks are depicted as lines joining the nodes, and tasks themselves are represented as boxes, also known as nodes. A network diagram allows you to visualize project operations more like a flowchart style than a Gantt chart, which is a timescaled view. This is helpful if you want to focus more on the connections between tasks than on their lengths and order. Each node in the Network Diagram view has multiple fields containing task-related data.

The links between tasks are emphasized in the Network Diagram view. Project depicts summary tasks as parallelogram-shaped nodes and finished tasks as nodes with an X across them. Project offers many formatting options for the Network Diagram view, much like it does for Gantt chart views. To group nodes by time period, for instance, you can

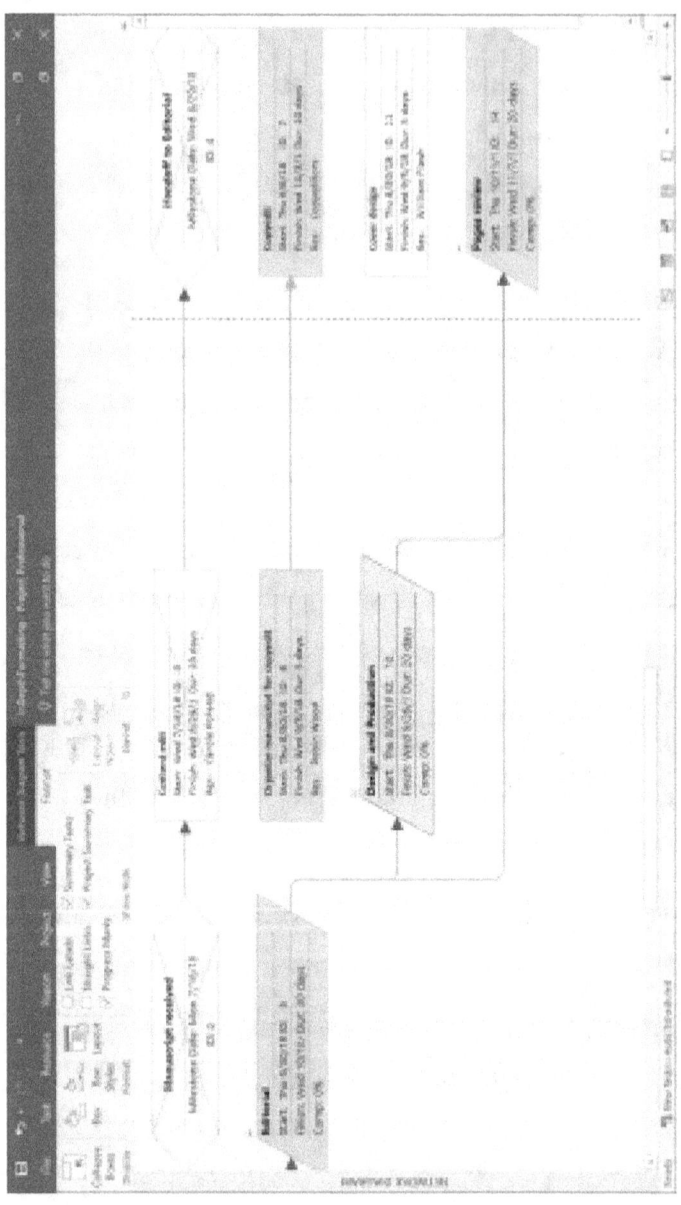

alter the Network Diagram view's general structure. You should look more closely at the formatting options if you use network diagrams frequently. To alter the look of various node types, use the Box Styles dialog box, which can be accessed from the Format tab in the Format group while viewing a network diagram.

Project depicts summary tasks as parallelogram-shaped nodes and finished tasks as nodes with an X across them. Project offers many formatting options for the Network Diagram view, much like it does for Gantt chart views. To group nodes by time period, for instance, you can alter the Network Diagram view's general structure. You should look more closely at the formatting options if you use network diagrams frequently. To alter the look of various node types, use the Box Styles dialog box, which can be accessed from the Format tab in the Format group while viewing a network diagram. To modify the appearance and content of boxes (nodes) in the Network Diagram view, use the Box Styles dialog box. Because different box styles correspond to different task kinds, box styles in the Network Diagram view are comparable to bar styles in a Gantt chart. Data templates, box border formatting, and box background formatting are the three primary components of box styles. All of the box styles in the Network Diagram view are preset. You can change how the built-in box styles look (more particularly, how the border and background look), but you can't make your own.

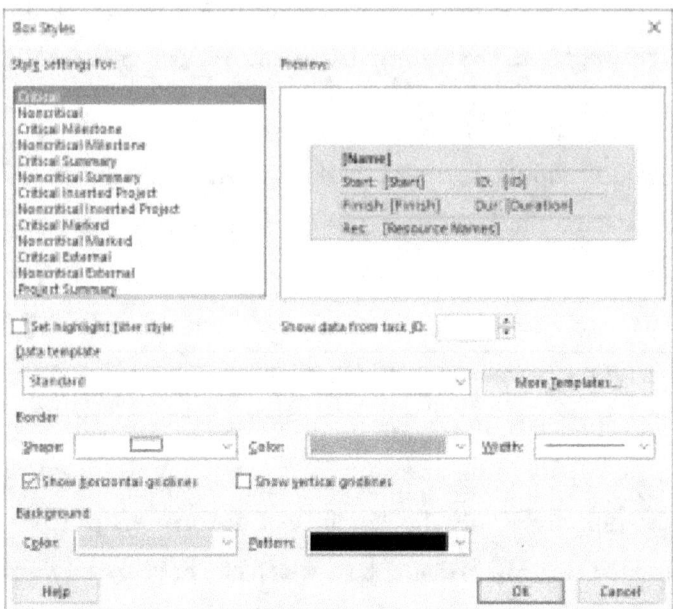

Because different box styles correspond to different task kinds, box styles in the Network Diagram view are comparable to bar styles in a Gantt chart. Data templates, box border formatting, and box background formatting are the three primary components of box styles. All of the box styles in the Network Diagram view are preset. You can change how the built-in box styles look (more particularly, how the border and background look), but you can't make your own. Project makes use of data templates like Standard and Summary for the Network Diagram view. In this case, templates control both the layout and the fields that show up in boxes (nodes). (Do not mix these templates with file templates.)

You have two options: either make your own template or use one of the pre-existing data templates in your Network Diagram view. For instance, you may make a template with the Work Breakdown Structure (WBS) code field for every task. The Data Template Definition dialog box is where you do this.

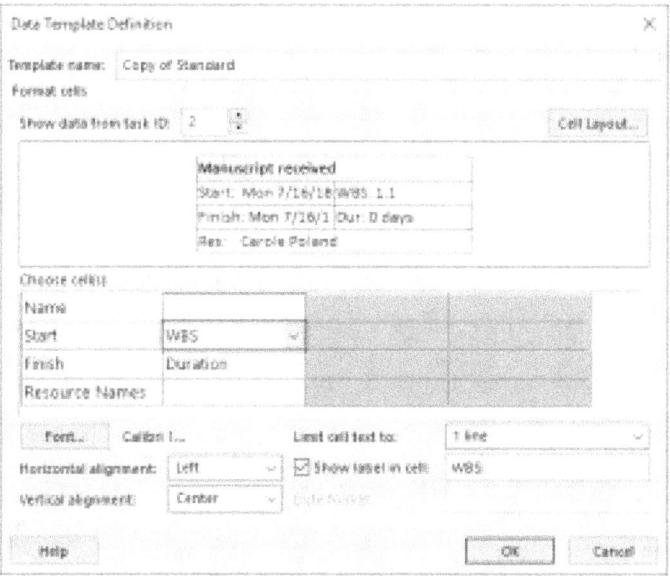

The Format tab has the following extra formatting buttons that are relevant to the Network Diagram view:

You can use the Box Styles button to format all of the boxes in the Network Diagram view, or you can use the Box button to format only the active box. When you have a Gantt chart view open, this is comparable to the Bar Styles and Bar buttons on the Format tab.

To manage things like the general placement of task boxes by time period, such week or month, use the Layout button. By checking the Link Labels check box, you can reveal or conceal the different kinds of task linkages, such Start to Start (SS), between tasks.

To explore more of the network, rapidly zoom out of the Network Diagram view using the Collapse Boxes button. To change the box style of a network diagram

- To see the Network Diagram view, select Network Diagram from the Task Views group on the View tab.
- To access the Box Styles dialog box, select Box Styles under the Format group on the Network Diagram Tools Format tab.
- Choose the box style you wish to change in the Style Settings For box.

- Choose the data template for which you wish to modify the box style from the list of data templates.
- Choose the color, shape, and any display settings you wish to use for this box design in the Border section.
- Choose your preferred color and pattern in the Background area.
- Press OK.

HOW TO MAKE OR ALTER A NETWORK DIAGRAM BOX DATA TEMPLATE (NODE)

- Launch the Box Styles dialog box in the Network Diagram view.
- To access the Data Templates dialog box, click More Templates. Either a new data template or a copy of an existing template can be created in this dialog box.

Take one of these actions:

- To build a new template, click New.
- To make a copy, choose a template and click Copy.
- To make changes to a template, select it and click Edit.
- Choose the desired choices in the Data Template Definition dialog box. To help you with your work, use the dialog box's task node preview.

- To exit the Data Template Definition dialog box, click OK. Then, to exit the Data Templates dialog box, click Close.
- Click OK after making sure your updated or new data template is selected in the Box Styles dialog box.

HOW TO CHANGE A PARTICULAR TASK BOX (NODE) IN THE DISPLAY OF THE NETWORK DIAGRAM

- Choose the task box you wish to edit in the Network Diagram view.
- To open the Format Box dialog box, select Box in the Format group on the Format tab.
- Choose the desired choices in the Format Box dialog box. Make use of the dialog box's preview to assist direct your work.
- Press OK.

CHAPTER ELEVEN
CREATE A CALENDAR VIEW FORMAT

One of the most basic views in Project is the Calendar view, which is similar to the Timeline view. When communicating schedule information with resources or stakeholders who would rather have a more thorough view, like the Gantt Chart view, or a more conventional "month-at-a-glance" format, this view is particularly helpful. The Calendar view shows tasks as bars spanning the days on which they are scheduled to occur, much like a conventional "month-at-a-glance" calendar.

Several weeks are shown at a time in this view. The orange blocks in the monthly calendars on the left side of the picture represent the viewable weeks. The Calendar view can be style-based formatted in Project, just like other views. In the Calendar view, you can alter how each instance of a specific item type looks. You can, for instance, make every activity on the important path in the plan seem red.

HOW TO MODIFY WEEK HEIGHT

- Make the Calendar view visible.
- Select Adjust Week Height from the Layout group on the Format tab.

PRINTING

Project provides more customization choices for printing views. You may need to modify details for the views you print because views like the Gantt Chart view are frequently shared with resources and other project stakeholders.

Project printing is comparable to printing in other Office applications. However, Project has different parameters. The ability to print data for a certain date range is a useful print setting in Project. For instance, in a Gantt chart view, Project will print the table section of the view as it is now configured, followed by only the date range you designate from the chart section of the view.

Depending on the view type that is now shown, you can change the printing and page layout settings. Compared to more complicated views, such as the Gantt Chart view, simpler views, such as the Resource Sheet view, offer less options for printing and page layout. These variations are visible in the Page Setup dialog box. Depending on the active view, different options are accessible on the Legend and View tabs. Examples of how the page configuration options can change are as follows:

- You can adjust the timescale to fit the page for Gantt charts and usage views.
- You have the option to add row and column totals for use views.
- For sheet views like the Task Sheet or Resource Sheet view, the Legend tab is not accessible.

Microsoft Project Bible

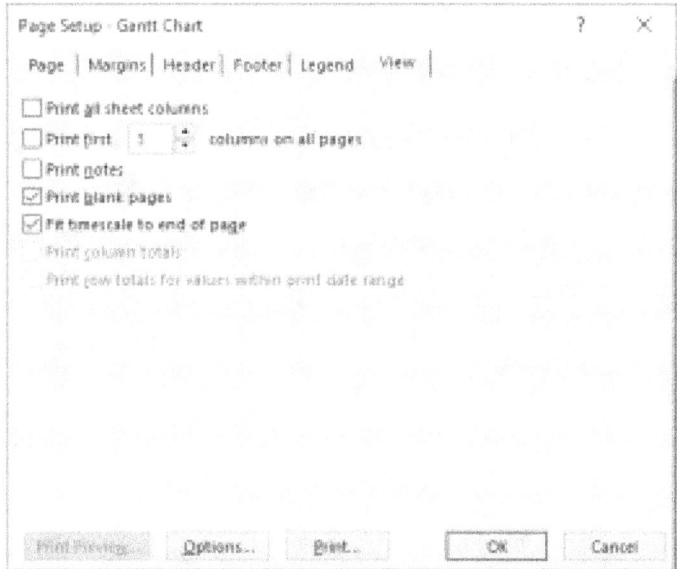

You have a lot of options when printing the majority of view kinds. For instance, you can add particular options like task or resource notes, alter headers and footers, and choose what will appear in the legend. The caption that is printed with a Gantt chart view is one item that is frequently customized during printing. This is done on the Page Setup dialog box's Legend tab. The project title and other general things can be added to the legend, as field values like the plan's total cost (which is entered in the Cost field). The Total Cost value for the plan is included in this personalized legend in the Page Setup dialog box. A glimpse of the field codes and other text in the Left, Center, and Right tabs can be found on the legend tab. An image can even be added to the legend.

To add precisely the information, you choose to your printed views, explore the Legend options. Sharing a glimpse of a Project perspective with those who may not have Project may be necessary at times. Project facilitates the simple creation of PDF and XPS format files in order to do this. All of the page setup settings covered in this chapter apply when creating PDF or XPS output files since you "print" to them just like you would when printing to a printer.

HOW TO CHANGE THE PRINT SETTINGS

- Set up the view and display it as you would like it to appear on the printing. For instance, you can change the timescale and viewable columns in a Gantt chart view.
- To see the Print page with the current view in the preview, click the File tab first, followed by the Backstage view.
- Choose the desired print settings in the Settings area. Make use of the preview as a guide for your work.

HOW TO MODIFY VIEW-SPECIFIC SETTINGS

- Set up the view and display it as you would like it to appear on the printing.
- Show the Backstage view's Print page.
- To access the Page Setup dialog box, click the Page Setup link located to the left of the print preview at the bottom of the Settings section.
- The Legend and View tabs display the view-specific settings. After making your selections, click OK.

HOW TO ALTER THE HEADER OR FOOTER OF A VIEW

- Set up the view and display it as you would like it to appear on the printing.

- Show the Backstage view's Print page.
- To access the Page Setup dialog box, choose Page Setup in the Settings section.
- Click OK after making your selections on the Header and Footer sections.

HOW TO CREATE AN XPS OR PDF FILE

- Set up the view and display it as you would like it to appear on the printing.
- To see the Export page, click Export after selecting the File tab to see the Backstage view.
- Select "Create XPS/PDF Document."
- Click Create PDF/XPS to bring up the Browse dialog box on the right side of the page.
- Enter the desired file name and choose the location to save the file.
- Click OK to open the Document Export Options dialog box after choosing either PDF Files or XPS Files in the Save as type box, depending on the format you prefer.
- Click OK after choosing the desired date range and other settings in the Document Export Options dialog box.

MAKE A UNIQUE REPORT

A custom report can be thought of as a container for any combination of these components:

- Diagrams Include charts of the bar, area, or other kinds in a report.
- Tables To display data in a row-and-column manner, use tables.
- Pictures Include pictures in a report, such as JPEG or PNG files.
- Forms: Add and modify pre-made forms like circles, speech bubbles, and arrows. In a report, shapes are a wonderful way to highlight key information.
- Text fields: Anywhere on a report, add a text box.

The Insert group on the Report Tools Design tab has the buttons to add these components to a report. To add components to a report, use the buttons in the Insert group of the Report Tools Design Tab. Utilize these capabilities in a Project report in the same way that you would in an Excel workbook or a PowerPoint presentation, or any other Microsoft Office document.

Tables and charts are distinct from the other components of the report. Task and resource field data from Project's open plan are used in charts and tables. As the plan's underlying data changes, the field values in a chart or table will also immediately update. You can choose which report elements to start with when you create a new report. You can choose which elements to include while making a new report. With these choices, you can begin with a report that is blank or one that has a preliminary table or chart. Two similar charts are included in a new report created via the Comparison option, which assumes that you will alter one or both of them. It doesn't really matter which components you use when building a new report because it's simple to add more to a custom report.

You should probably begin by constructing a table, chart, or both to present the critical information from your strategy, and then embellishing or decorating the charts and tables with text boxes, pictures, or forms to highlight or embellish your main points. Project opens the Field List window when you add or modify a table or chart in a report. You can use this pane to manage which plan data are shown in the chosen table or chart and how they are arranged.

The Field List pane for the chosen table or chart (as seen above) opens in this custom report.

Task fields and resource fields are the two categories into which the Field List pane divides fields. For convenience, the fields that are presently selected are indicated at the bottom of the field list.

Options to filter, group, outline, or order the selected fields are located at the bottom of the Field List pane. To manage how the chosen fields appear in reports, use these settings.

Here are some examples of how you can manage the organization of report data:

Set Outline Level to Level 1 to display only the top-level summary task cost values in a pie chart with task cost fields. Use the Milestones filter to display only milestone tasks in a table with task fields. Sort the resources' remaining work values in a table by Remaining Work in decreasing order.

A collection of educational resources in the form of reports is part of the project. Click Getting Started, then Click Get Started With Project in the View Reports group on the Report tab. Additional details on reports can also be found in the Project online support. Click Get Help after entering "Create a Project report" in the Tell Me box.

HOW VIEWS AND REPORTING COMPARE

Let's contrast the reports and view. Every report or view only looks at a portion of the data in your plan. Each view and report that comes with Project is intended to assist you in better visualizing a certain element of your strategy. To manage the elements of your plan that are most important to you, you typically need to deal with a variety of reports and views across time. Working with timescaled views, such as the Gantt chart views, the Timeline and usage views, and reports, such as Upcoming Tasks, Critical Tasks, and Late Tasks, can provide you with the best understanding of your plan, for instance, if your project is predominantly deadline-driven. However, there are significant distinctions between reports and opinions. You have worked in views throughout this book to see schedule information (such which resources are assigned to which tasks) as well as to add and change schedule data (like task names and resource assignments).

However, you are unable to directly alter the data in your plan while using reports. For instance, you are unable to alter resource assignments or add or remove tasks. Reports are excellent at providing you with more options for identifying and disseminating important elements of your plan in aesthetically appealing formats. Furthermore, reports can be tailored to contain only the data you like and to be shown in the manner of your choice.

Not available in other plans, custom reports are only available in the plan in which they were developed. You can use the Organizer to copy a custom report to the Global template, which will be available in any plan you work on in Project.

HOW TO PRODUCE A NEW REPORT

- Select New Report from the View Reports group on the Report tab.
- Decide if you want a new report that is blank or includes additional elements.
- Type a name into the Report Name dialog box, then select OK. In order for you to read this report later, this name will be the title at the top of the report and will show up in the Custom list (on the Report tab, in the read Reports group).

HOW TO INCLUDE A CHART IN A REPORT

- To open the Insert Chart dialog box, select Chart from the Insert group on the Report Tools Design tab.
- Choose the desired chart type and then the desired chart layout from the options on the left side of the dialog box. Click OK after that. The Field List window is displayed and the new chart is added to the report by Project.
- To move the chart to the desired location on the report, drag it.

HOW TO INCLUDE A TABLE IN A REPORT

- Select Table from the Insert group on the Report Tools Design tab.
- To move the table to the desired location on the report, drag it.

HOW TO INCLUDE A TEXT FIELD IN A REPORT

- Select Text Box under the Insert group on the Report Tools Design tab.
- Click the location of the text box's upper-left corner in the report, then drag it down and to the right until it appears the way you want it to. Next, let go of the mouse button.
- Type the desired text into the text box.
- Choose other text formatting options from the Drawing Tools Format tab and the Font group on the Task tab.

HOW TO GIVE A REPORT A SHAPE

- Select Shapes from the Insert category on the Report Tools Design tab.
- Select the desired form by clicking on it in the Shapes list.
- To construct and resize the shape in the report, click and drag.

- If desired, add text to the object and use any other formatting options from the Font group on the Task tab and the Drawing Tools Format tab.

HOW TO INCLUDE A PICTURE IN A REPORT

- Select Images from the Insert group on the Report Tools Design tab.
- Click Open after selecting the image you wish to include in the report. You can use the Picture Tools Format buttons to further alter the image after it has been inserted, as well as move and resize it.

PERSONALIZE A REPORT'S CHARTS

You can chart using Project's reports in a manner similar to that of spreadsheet programs like Microsoft Excel. You may make many different kinds of charts with Project, including as pie, bar, line, and column charts. As previously indicated, the Field List window opens and two Chart Tools tabs show up on the ribbon when you add a chart or select one in a report.

Here is a description of the Design and Format tabs:

- The tab for Design To add components like data labels and alter the chart's layout and style, use the buttons on this tab.

- The tab for Format Data series and other chart

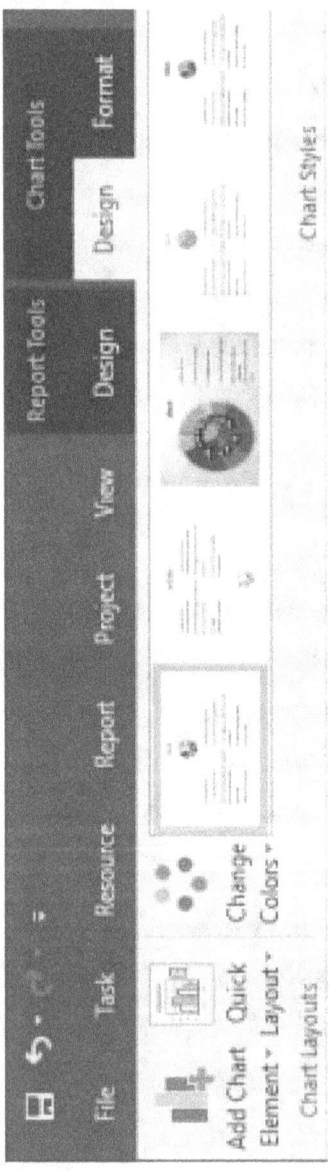

elements can be formatted using the buttons on this tab.

Additionally, three buttons show up to the right of each chart when you pick it. When you add or pick a chart, the buttons for Chart Elements, Chart Styles, and Chart Filters become available.

The following buttons can be used to further refine your chart:

- Elements of a Chart Add or remove components, like data labels, quickly.
- Styles of Charts: Alter the chart's color scheme and select a different chart style, including color and fill combinations.
- Filters for Charts: Add or remove the particular data categories (which relate to particular activities or resources) and data series (which correspond to Project fields).

These three buttons provide you easy access to some of the options on the Chart Tools Design tab. The Field List window opens when you pick a chart in a report, as mentioned in the preceding subject.

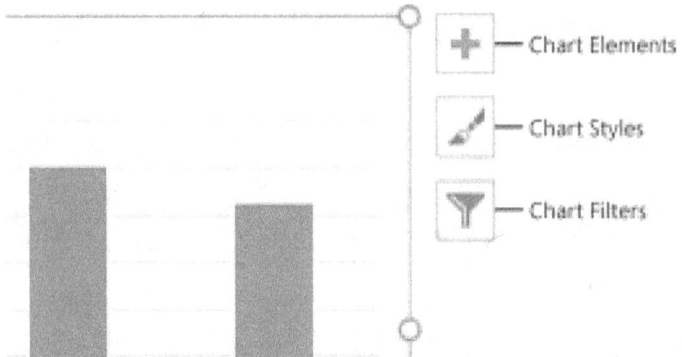

Let's examine the contents of the Field List window for charts in greater detail:

- Activities or Materials: Decide what kind of data you wish to use. Data from Task or Resource fields can be shown in a chart.
- Classification: Select the main object that will be charted. Descriptive attributes such as task ID and task name are among the categories that are available while working with task data. Attributes such as the resource name are included in resource data categories. Both task and resource data can be found in some categories, such as time. The category dictates which field labels are displayed on the x-axis when dealing with a bar or line chart.
- Fields available: Types of fields, such Cost and Work, are arranged in an outline. To view the fields

in each field category, expand it. Specific fields For convenience, the fields that are presently selected are indicated at the bottom of the field list.

FEATURES FOR ORGANIZING DATA (FILTER, GROUP BY, ETC.)

To manage how the task or resource data is displayed on the chart, use these settings. For instance, you can filter resources to display just resources that are generally located or organize activities according to key tasks. You have a lot of options when creating charts with the Field List pane. You may view your findings in the chart as soon as you make changes in the Field List window. Choosing which project data to include in a graphic.

- Pick out the chart.
- Select Tasks or Resources as the data type you wish to deal with in the Field List pane.
- Choose the data category that will be charted from the Select Category list. For example, the task name for tasks or the resource name for resources.
- Choose the check boxes for the fields you wish to have in the chart in the Select Fields box. If you

choose Time as a category, an Edit button will show up so you may change the time settings.

ADVICE

At the bottom of the Select Fields box are the names of the fields that have been selected. Drag the chosen field names up or down to change the fields' order as they show in the chart. Additionally, you can alter or remove a field name by right-clicking on it.

- Choose any filter or other settings you wish to apply to the tasks or resources at the bottom of the Field List pane.
- Click the Chart Filters icon to the right of the chart to further modify its content. Then, you can fine-tune the series (the particular data to be tracked) and categories (the labels on the x-axis) until the chart looks the way you want it to.

The process of creating a chart can be somewhat iterative. The chart instantly adjusts in accordance with your changes to its settings. The Field List and other settings of the built-in charts in Project can also be examined, and the same outcomes can be produced in your own charts.

HOW TO ALTER THE STYLE AND FORMAT OF A CHART

- Pick out the chart.
- Choose the desired chart type, elements, and further settings on the Chart Tools Format tab.
- Choose your preferred layout, color, or style from the Chart Tools Design menu.

Additionally, you may modify the series and category data or apply format and design options using the three floating chart buttons. For instance, if the particular chart element you wish to format is not there in the chart, click the Chart Elements button and then add it. This button can also be used to eliminate components that you don't want.

PERSONALIZE A REPORT'S TABLES

Similar to views, tables in reports display field values in the rows and use Project field labels as column headings. You will see the identical field labels (like Duration) and values (like 20 days) in all of Project's views and dialog boxes. Two Table Tools tabs show up on the ribbon when you pick a table in a report. When you add or select a table, the Design and Layout tabs of the Table Tools are displayed. Here is a description of the Design and Layout tabs:

- The tab for Design To add or delete a header row, modify the table's formatting, apply table styles (color schemes), and apply WordArt styles to specific table text, use the buttons on this tab.
- The tab for Layout Adjust the table's cell content alignment, row height, column width, and other table size settings using the buttons on this tab.
- The Field List window opens when you pick any table in a report, just like it does with charts. You have control over which fields appear in the chosen table in this window. You can also apply filtering, grouping, and sorting to the table rows in the Field List pane. You can also adjust the outline levels for task fields to control which tasks are shown.
- Task fields and resource fields are the two categories into which Project fields are arranged. The Select Category box does not show up for tables because these groups are only applicable to charts.

A table's column arrangement, from left to right, is determined by the order in which fields are added. The names of the fields you add show up at the bottom of the Select Fields box. Drag the field names up or down to rearrange the table's columns. The table changes to reflect the outcome as you do this.

Microsoft Project Bible

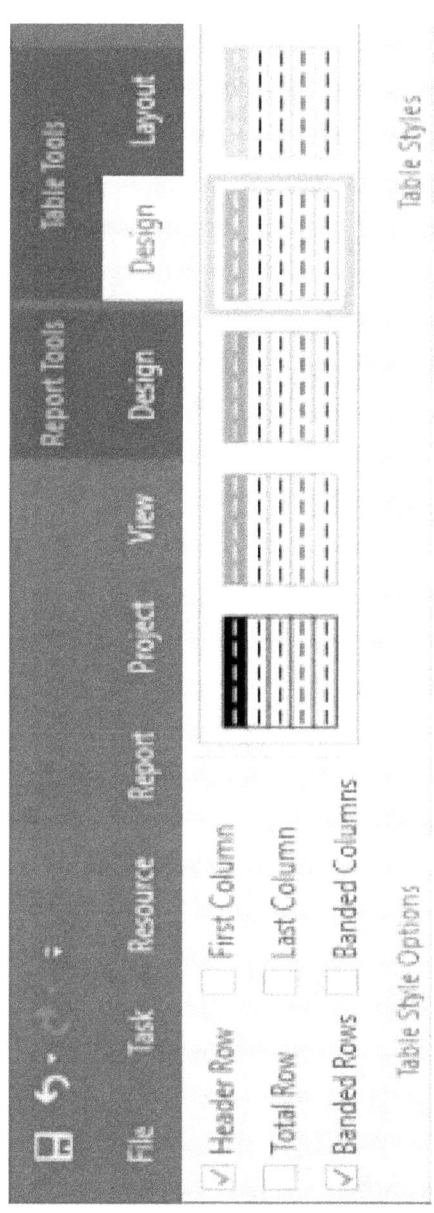

Similar to the features you use in view-based tables, the Field List pane's bottom contains options to filter, organize, or sort the table data. Resources lack an outline structure, hence the Outline Level box is only accessible when working with task fields.

- Choose the table in order to choose which project data to include in it.
- Select the data type you wish to deal with in the Field List pane: Activities or Materials.
- Choose the check boxes for the fields you wish to have in the table in the Select Fields window. You have two options: drag the field names you've chosen up or down at the bottom of the Select Fields box, or select the fields in the order you want them to appear, from left to right.
- Use the filter, group, sort, or (for task fields) outline level options at the bottom of the Field List window to further modify the table's content.

HOW TO ALTER THE LAYOUT AND DESIGN OF A TABLE

- Decide on a table.
- Choose the desired size, alignment, and other settings on the Table Tools Layout tab.

- Choose the desired style options from the Table Tools Design menu.

CHAPTER TWELVE
MODIFY THE PROJECT

Project utilizes the ribbon interface, which provides good customization options, like the majority of Microsoft Office applications. Other customization capabilities that are specific to Project include the global template and organizer. Additionally, Project offers customization tools that are comparable to those found in other Office applications, such as the ability to record Microsoft Visual Basic for Applications (VBA) macros.

The built-in views, tables, reports, and other components that you see in Project are provided by a global template called Global.mpt. A view, table, or other similar element is immediately copied from the global template to the plan the first time it is displayed in that plan. The element then becomes part of the plan. Any further modifications made to that plan element (such as altering the fields shown in a table) solely apply to that particular plan and have no impact on the global template. Although you often don't deal directly with the global template, it is installed as part of Project.

First, the global template contains the detailed definitions of all views, tables, and other components. For instance, the global template determines which set of fields are present in the default Usage table and which are not. The following are among the elements that the global template provides: Views, Reports, Tables, Filters, Calendars, Teams, Modules (VBA macros), import/export maps, and custom fields can also be copied to the global template or between plans.

A view or other built-in element that has been customized stays in the plan in which it was altered. With views and tables, you can use your own unique view or table in place of the version of that element in the global template. But if you make a new element, like a new view, it is copied to the global template and then appears in all the other plans you might possibly use. You can alter this behavior if you don't want a new element to be copied to your global template. Calendars, however, are an exception. When a bespoke calendar is made, it stays entirely inside the original plan. Working times in other plans may be redefined in ways you did not intend by a modified standard calendar that satisfies your needs in one plan. Because of this, Project offers a feature that allows you to safely transfer custom calendars (as well as other aspects) between plans. The Organizer is that feature.

The names of the tabs in the Organizer dialog box represent the full range of elements you can use the Organizer to copy across plans.

You can copy components between plans or between a plan and the global template in the Organizer dialog box. components from the global template are shown on the left side of the dialog box, while components that have been utilized in the active plan at any point (like views presented) are shown on the right. This is the pattern for the majority of the Organizer dialog box's tabs.

To duplicate elements between a plan and the global template, use the tabs and both sides of the Organizer dialog box. As an alternative, you can duplicate elements between plans by choosing a different open plan instead of the global template. An element can be copied to the plan indicated on the right by selecting it on the left side of the dialog box and then clicking the Copy button. The global template, by default, is the file presented on the left when an element on the right side of the dialog box is selected and subsequently copied by clicking the Copy button.

Microsoft Project Bible

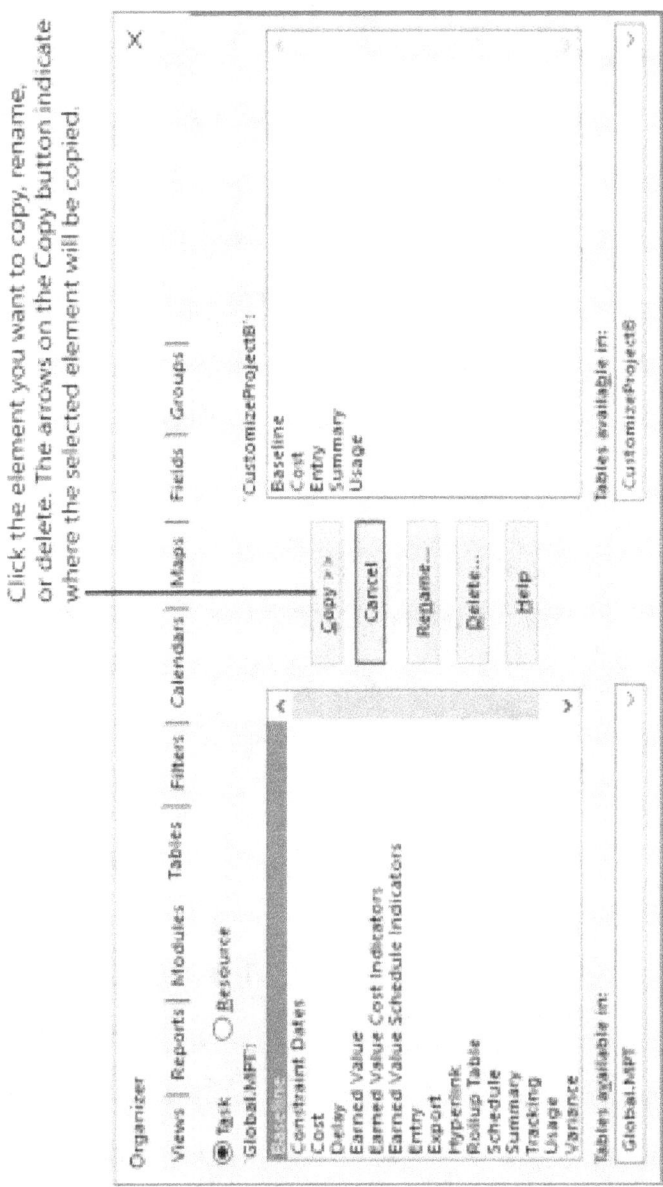

HOW TO DUPLICATE A COMPONENT OF TWO DESIGNS

- First, open the two designs you wish to duplicate an element from.
- To enter the Organizer dialog box, click Info after selecting the File tab to show the Backstage view.
- Click the names of the plans you wish to duplicate an element between in the Elements available in boxes at the bottom of the Organizer dialog box.
- Next, select the element type tab that you wish to duplicate.
- Choose the element you wish to duplicate from its plan to the other plan from the options on the left or right side of the Organizer dialog box. To copy an element, you may need to first click Task or Resource in the Tables, Filters, Fields, or Groups tab. When you pick an element on either side of the dialog box, the two arrow symbols on the Copy button change direction and point in the direction of the plan to which the selected element will be copied.
- Press the Copy icon.
- To exit the Organizer dialog box, click Close.

HOW TO TRANSFER A PERSONALIZED COMPONENT TO THE GLOBAL TEMPLATE

- Launch the plan with the personalized component.
- The Organizer dialog box will open.
- Select the element type tab that you wish to duplicate.
- Confirm that the dialog box's left side displays Global.MPT. If not, choose Global.MPT from the Elements available in box on the dialog box's left side.
- Choose the custom element you wish to copy to the global template from the dialog box's right side. When you pick an element on the right side of the dialog box, the two arrow symbols (>>) on the Copy button change direction (<<).
- Press the Copy icon.
- To exit the Organizer dialog box, click Close.

HOW TO STOP THE GLOBAL TEMPLATE FROM AUTOMATICALLY ADDING CUSTOMIZED ELEMENTS

- To enter the Project Options dialog box, click Options after selecting the File tab to show the Backstage view.

- The Advanced page will appear.
- Click OK after checking the box to "Automatically Add New Views, Tables, Filters, and Groups to the global" under Display.

RECORD AND EXECUTE MACROS

There may be a lot of repeated tasks in Project. You can save time by creating a macro that records mouse movements and keystrokes for subsequent playback. Office's built-in macro programming language, Visual Basic for Applications (VBA), is used to record the macro. Although VBA allows you to execute complex tasks, you can record and replay basic macros without ever seeing or interacting with VBA code.

Which repetitious tasks would you like to record in a macro? Here's an illustration. One of the best ways to communicate project data to others is to create a graphic-image snapshot of a view. However, as the plan is changed, it's possible that the information you initially record will soon become outdated. Taking updated snapshots can be a tedious process that is best automated with a macro. You can quickly create a new GIF picture snapshot of a plan and save it to a file when this activity is automated. From there, you can distribute the GIF image file in different ways, like attaching it to an email or publishing it to a website or document. By default, the global template contains the macros you define. You may always access the global template's macros in Project since it is open when Project is operating. To run the macro in additional plans, the original plan for which you developed it does not have to be open. Additionally, you can copy macros between plans using the Organizer.

To send it to a friend, for instance, you can use the Organizer to copy a VBA module that includes the macro from the global template to a different plan. If you keep a macro in a plan, you can use it in any plan as long as the plan containing the macro is open. The Record Macro dialog box is where you initially enter information about the macro before you start recording it.

You provide a name and other details in the Record Macro dialog box when you record a new macro. Macro names cannot contain spaces and must start with a letter. An underscore (_) can be used in place of a space to make your macro names easier to understand. For instance, you may call a macro Capture_GIF_Image instead of CaptureGIFImage. You can designate a keyboard shortcut key for a macro when you record it. Combinations like Ctrl+F (the keyboard shortcut for Find) and Ctrl+G (Go To) are not available because you cannot use a Ctrl+ combination that Project has already reserved.

When you record a macro, Project does not actually capture and replay every mouse click and second that passes. Rather,

Project merely logs the outcomes of your mouse and keystroke movements. Do not feel pressured to finish the macro recording in a hurry. Once a macro has been recorded, it can be executed using the Macros dialog box or, if you have designated a shortcut key, by pressing it.

Microsoft Project Bible

HOW TO CAPTURE A MACRO

- To open the Record Macro dialog box, click the Macros arrow in the Macros group on the View tab. Next, click Record Macro.

- Click OK after entering a name, description, and any other desired information. The new macro is being recorded by the project.

- Take the actions you wish to have the macro record.
- When you're prepared to end the macro's recording, click the Macros arrow in the Macros group on the View tab, and then select Stop Recording.
- Click Macros in the Macros group on the View tab to launch the Macros dialog box.
- Select a macro name in the Macro name box, and then select Run.

ADVICE

You can also execute the macro by pressing its key combination if you gave it a Ctrl+ keyboard shortcut.

HOW TO REMOVE A MACRO

- Launch the dialog box for macros.
- Select a macro name in the Macro name box, and then select Delete.
- Click Close after confirming the deletion.

MODIFY MACROS

Once a macro has been recorded, it may function flawlessly as planned or it may require some code modifications. You can add functionality to the macro, such dismissing an alarm, by modifying its code. This is something you can't do when recording the macro. The code for a macro is stored in a VBA module, and the VBA environment—also known as the Visual Basic Editor—is where you work with the code.

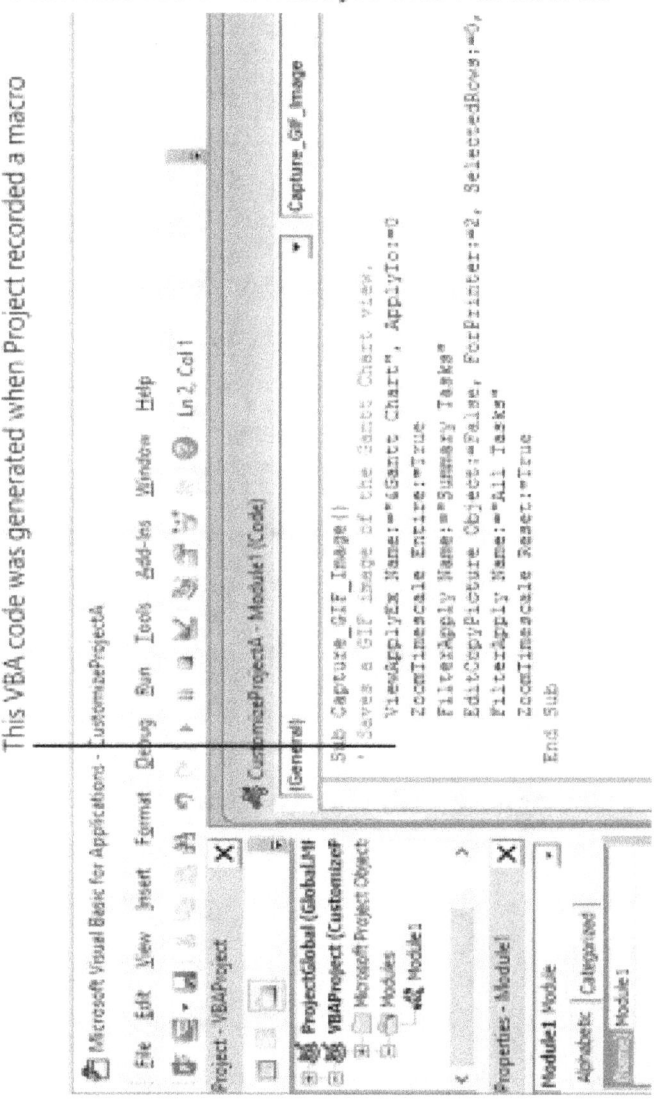

This VBA code was generated when Project recorded a macro

If you look at the code for the VBA module, you may see certain code values like FilterApply (which applies a filter) and EditCopyPicture (which copies a photo) that match any actions you entered in the macro. Although a thorough description of the VBA language is outside the purview of this book, here is an illustration of how powerful VBA is for task automation. Suppose you've recorded a macro that saves a view's GIF image file. When you first save the document while recording the macro, everything goes smoothly. However, a dialog box asking you to confirm that you want to replace the current GIF image file with a file of the same name appears when you try to execute the macro again. To prevent the interruption each time you execute the macro, you can use a single line of VBA code.

An additional line of code in this sample code from a recorded macro prevents a dialog box from displaying. This line of code conceals the dialog box that appears when you run the macro in the example GIF image file. Rather, the macro makes Project accept the default setting of substituting a GIF image file with the same name for the current one.

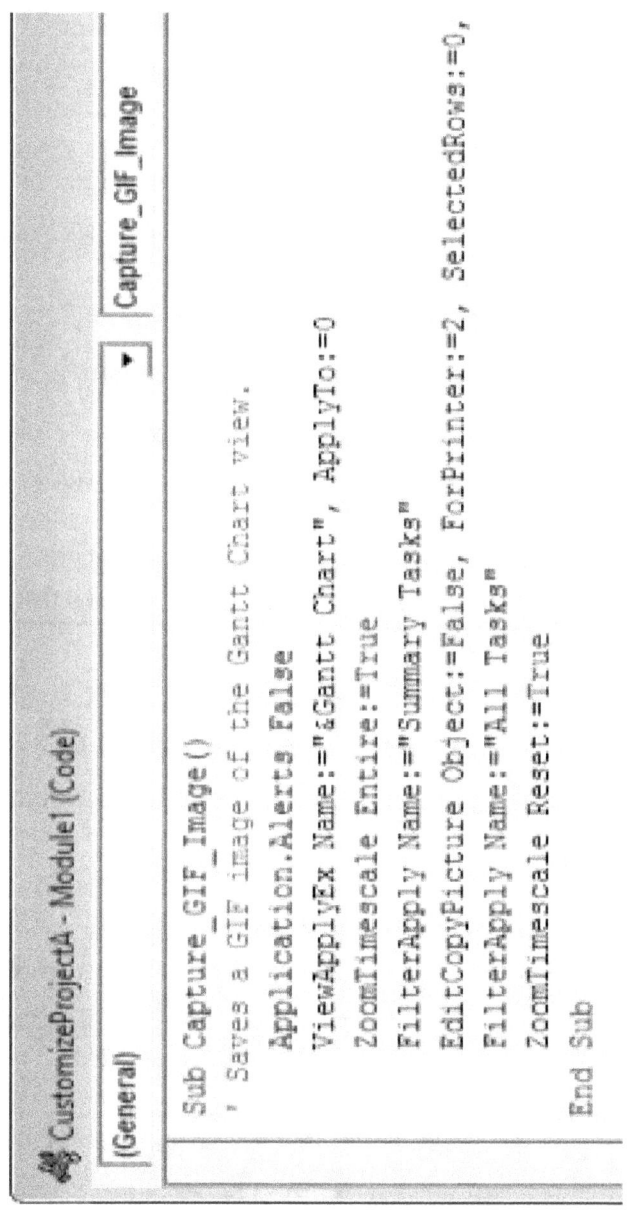

HOW TO MAKE CHANGES TO A MACRO

- Click Macros under the Macros group on the View tab.
- After selecting a macro's name, select Edit. In the Visual Basic Editor, Project loads the module containing the macro.
- Modify the code in VBA.
- Click Close and Return to Microsoft Project from the Visual Basic Editor's File menu after you're finished altering the macro. You go back to the plan as the Visual Basic Editor shuts.

PERSONALIZE THE QUICK ACCESS TOOLBAR AND RIBBON

You have a number of options when it comes to using Project, just like with other Office applications. The following are just a few of the numerous customization options:

- Add commands that are often used to the Quick Access Toolbar. Customize the ribbon's commands.
- A personalized tab with a personalized command and a personalized Quick Access Toolbar.

In most cases, you can customize the Quick Access Toolbar and ribbon regardless of the plan you have open in Project.

If you'd like, you can restrict access to a personalized Quick Access Toolbar to a particular plan. The Quick Access Toolbar can be customized in a number of ways: Click Add To Quick Access Toolbar from the shortcut menu that displays when you right-click any command on the ribbon.

After selecting the Customize Quick Access Toolbar launcher, select a command from the list of frequently used commands. To add, rearrange, or remove commands from the Quick Access Toolbar, use the Project Options dialog box.

To add, remove, or rearrange commands on the Quick Access Toolbar, use the Project Options dialog box's Quick Access Toolbar page. The ribbon can be customized using the Customize Ribbon page in the same Project Options dialog box.

To alter the ribbon, use the Project Options dialog box's Customize Ribbon page. You can add or remove instructions from any tab or create additional tabs on the Customize Ribbon page. Additionally, you can use a single command in the Project Options dialog box to undo all adjustments from the ribbon or Quick Access Toolbar and restore them to their original state.

A personalized ribbon can be shared with other Project users. The Import/Export command is available for this purpose on the Customize Ribbon page of the Project Options dialog box. One command can be swiftly added to or removed from the Quick Access Toolbar 1. Take one of the following actions:

- You can right-click a command to add it to the Quick Access Toolbar. After it shows up on the ribbon, select Add to Quick Access Toolbar. Right-click the command where it appears in the Quick Access Toolbar, then select Remove From Quick Access Toolbar from the shortcut menu that displays. This will remove the command from the Quick Access Toolbar.

The Quick Access Toolbar can be customized

- To enter the Project Options dialog box, click Options after selecting the File tab to show the Backstage view.
- Open the Quick Access Toolbar page in the Project Options dialog box.

The Quick Access Toolbar page of the Project Options dialog box can also be viewed by clicking the arrow at the right end of the Quick Access Toolbar and then selecting More Commands.

- Choose the desired category of instructions from the Choose commands from box on the left side of the dialog box.
- All of the plans you work with in Project are automatically covered by the Quick Access Toolbar. Click the name of the plan you want the modified Quick Access Toolbar to apply to in the Customize Quick Access Toolbar box to make it only apply to that particular open plan.
- Click the Add button after choosing the command you wish to add to the Quick Access Toolbar from the list of available commands (in the big box on the left side of the dialog box).
- Choose a command from the list of Quick Access Toolbar commands (in the big box on the right side of the dialog box) and then move it using the up and down arrow buttons to the right of the box to rearrange the commands on the Quick Access Toolbar.
- Click OK once your customization is complete.

To return to the Quick Access Toolbar's initial state

- Click the Reset button on the Project Options dialog box's Quick Access Toolbar page, and then select Reset Only Quick Access Toolbar.

HOW TO PERSONALIZE THE RIBBON

- Open the Customize Ribbon page in the Project Options dialog box. The Customize Ribbon page of the Project Options dialog box can also be accessed by right-clicking the ribbon and selecting Customize The Ribbon.

Make any of the modifications listed below:

- In the list of ribbon commands (in the big box on the right side of the dialog box), pick a command, and then use the up and down arrow buttons to the right of the box to move it around to change the order of the commands on a particular tab.

To delete a command from the ribbon commands list (located on the dialog box's right side), take one of the following actions:

- Click the "Remove" button after selecting the command.
- To remove the command, right-click on it and select Remove from the shortcut menu that displays.

- Click the New Tab or New Group button to add a new tab or group to the current tab. Then, to give the new tab or group a name, click the Rename icon.

- Choose the group for the custom tab (located on the right side of the dialog box) before adding a command to it. Next, select a command from the list of possible commands (located on the dialog box's left side) and press the Add button.

It is not possible to rearrange or delete commands that are dimmed on the Customize Ribbon page.

- Click OK once your customization is complete.

HOW TO RESTORE THE RIBBON'S ORIGINAL LOOK

Perform one of the following actions on the Project Options dialog box's Customize Ribbon page:

- Click Reset, then Reset Only Selected Ribbon Tab. To restore a tab's original look, choose the tab from the list of ribbon commands (located on the right side of the dialog box).

- Click the Reset button, followed by Reset All Customizations, to restore the entire ribbon to its

- initial state. Additionally, the Quick Access Toolbar will be reset by this action.

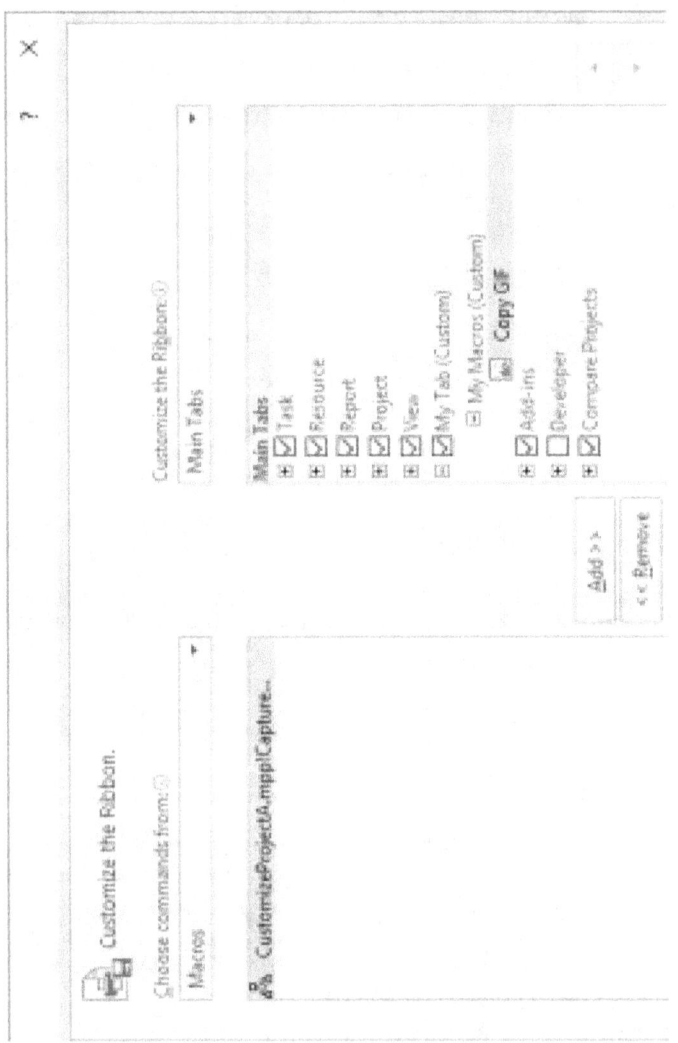

CHAPTER THIRTEEN
EXCHANGING DATA WITH OTHER PROGRAMS

You can copy Project data to and from another program. Project provides a number of options for importing and exporting data in addition to the typical copy and paste functions found in Microsoft Office, which you may already be familiar with.

The following terms will be used throughout this chapter:

The software that you are copying information from is known as the **source program**. The application to which you paste data is known as the **target program**.

Information can be copied from Project and pasted into it. There are a few things to keep in mind, though, because project information is very structured. You have a few choices about the outcomes when you copy data from Project (the source application) into other (destination) programs:

Task names, dates, and other information can be copied from a table in Project and pasted as structured tabular data in spreadsheet applications like Excel or as a table in word processing applications like Microsoft Word that support tables. A summary and subtask hierarchy are included in this project's selected data. The subtasks' indentation will typically reflect the summary/subtask hierarchy, and the column titles of the table containing the data you copied will typically also be pasted.

When you paste into Word, a structured table is created that maintains the Project summary task and subtask outline structure as well as the column titles. Text from a table in Project can be copied and pasted as tab-delimited text in WordPad or Notepad, two text editing programs that do not support tables.

If your email program supports HTML, you will likely see tabular results when pasting data from Project into it, like in Microsoft Outlook. The active view can be captured as a graphic-image snapshot, which can then be copied and pasted into any application that can handle graphic pictures.

ADVICE

A Paste Special capability is available in many Office applications, including Word, Excel, and PowerPoint. You have more alternatives when pasting data from Project into the destination program thanks to this feature. For instance, you can paste prepared or unformatted text or an image using Word's Paste Special feature. Additionally, you have the option to paste just the data or paste it along with a permanent link to the original data. The data in Project can be updated anytime the source data is modified when it is pasted in via a persistent link. Use the paste link option carefully and make sure you receive the desired results when entering data into calculated fields, like start and finish dates.

Two methods for choosing tabular data in Project are as follows:

- Click the range's upper-left corner, press and hold the Shift key, and then choose a range and then select the desired value by clicking on it in the lower-right corner of the range.
- In the top-left corner of a table, click the Select All button. Only cells with values will be copied, however the project chooses the complete table. Not every program handles pasting rich tabular data from Project in the same way. For instance, Project data pasted into Notepad would have tab-delimited data and no column headings. You can play around with this.

When pasting data into Project from other source programs, you additionally have the following options: A graphic image from another software can be pasted into a

Gantt Chart view's graphical section. A graphic can also be pasted into a report, a task, resource, or assignment note, or into a form view like the Task or Resource Form view. In Project, you can paste text into a table, like a list of task or resource names. You can paste a collection of cells from Excel or a set of paragraphs from Word into Project, for instance, or you can paste a list of task names arranged in a vertical column from Word or Excel into Project's Task Name column.

Planning is necessary when pasting text into Project in several columns. First, confirm that the columns in the Project table are in the same order as the information in the source program. The data in the source program can be rearranged to match the Project table's column order, or the other way around. Second, confirm that the data types supported by the columns in the source program (text, numbers, and dates, for instance) are the same as those supported by the columns in Project.

You can work with partial data if you need to paste a list of task or resource names into Project. If you just paste a list of task titles into Project, for instance, Project will schedule them to begin on the start date of the plan and assign them an approximate duration of one day. The scheduling information for the new tasks can then be updated as necessary.

To transfer Project's tabular data to a different application

- Arrange the data you wish to replicate in Project (for instance, navigate to the table with the desired fields).
- Click Copy in the Clipboard group on the Task tab after selecting the desired range of data. The chosen range is copied to the clipboard by the project.
- Paste the data after switching to the destination program. You can try pasting plain or prepared text if the destination program allows it.

PASTING TABULAR DATA INTO PROJECT FROM ANOTHER PROGRAM

- Choose the data you wish to paste into Project and copy it from the source program. Make that the tabular data is arranged in the proper field order required by Project if you need to duplicate more than one column.
- Select the column in a table that will hold the first value of the first row of the data to be pasted after switching to Project. Make sure the field order in the

Project table matches the arrangement of the copied data if you need to paste more than one column.

- Click Paste in the Clipboard group on the Task tab to paste the copied data. The data is pasted into the table by Project to import a graphic image into Project 1 from another application.
- To paste the image into Project, copy it from the source program.

Take any of these actions:

- Click the chart component of a Gantt chart view, and then select Paste from the Task tab's Clipboard group to paste the copied image into the chart portion. The image is pasted by Project. The image can then be resized or moved.
- Open or create a task or resource note, then paste the copied image into it. After clicking in the Notes field, hit Ctrl+V.
- Open the report before pasting the copied image into it. Make sure none of the report's elements are chosen by clicking in an empty section of it. Then, either click Paste on the Task tab's Clipboard group or press Ctrl+V.

Use Project to open files in different formats. There are many different sources of information that you can use to build a plan in Project. Examples include a resource list from a database or a task list from a spreadsheet. You may want to evaluate data from another program using Project's special features. For instance, many individuals use Excel to store simple task lists and to-do lists, but it is not practicable to account for fundamental scheduling concerns in Excel, such as differentiating between working and nonworking time. For one-time data sharing, you may find that just copying and pasting data into Project from other source apps is sufficient.

Sharing using a data file, however, can be a preferable choice if you need to exchange the same kind of data often or if its structure is too complicated for copying and pasting. Project employs maps, also known as import/export maps or data maps, to indicate the precise data to import or export and how to structure it when saving data to or opening data from files in various formats. To indicate how you want certain fields in the source program's file to match up with specific fields in the destination program's file, you utilize data maps.

An import/export map can be used again once it has been set up. To assist you in establishing the appropriate data map for the data you wish to import, Project has a function known as the Import Wizard.

Microsoft Project Bible

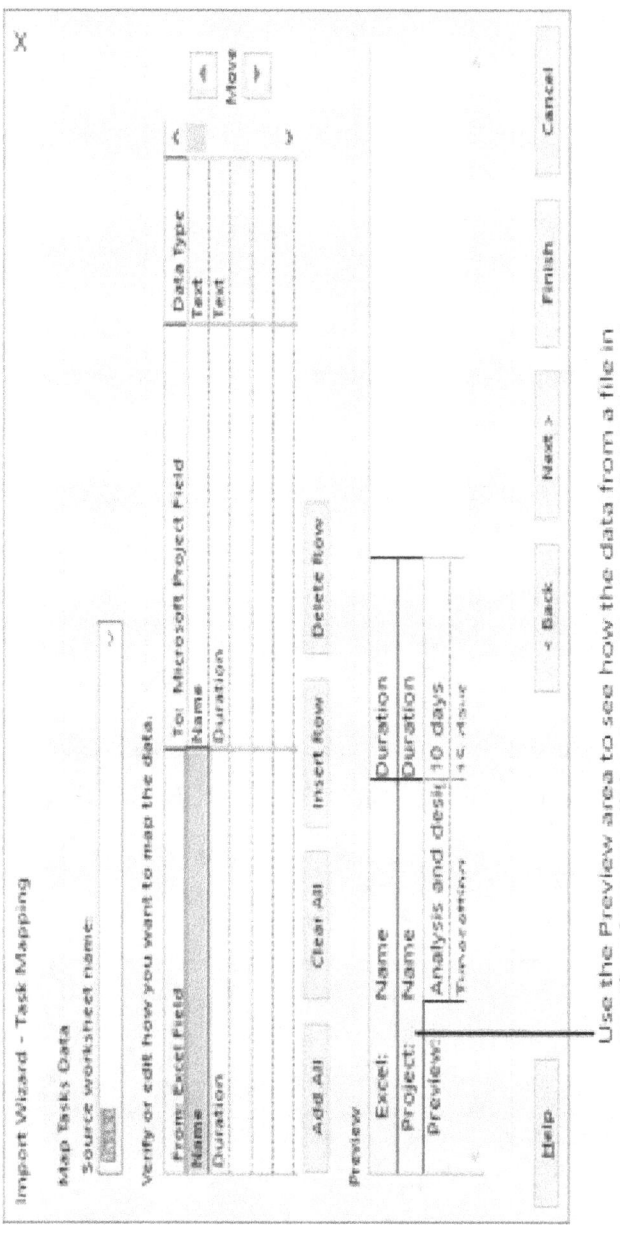

The Import Wizard organizes the process of importing structured data from another file format into Project using maps. For instance, when you import a task list from Excel, the Import Wizard displays the contents of the imported task list. You define how Project should import data from different file formats—in this example, an Excel workbook—on the Task Mapping page of the Import Wizard. The data is then prepared for more intricate tasks, including creating task linkages, after it has been imported.

HOW TO OPEN A FILE IN A DIFFERENT FORMAT

- Select the Backstage view by clicking the File tab, and then select Open.
- To open the file, click Browse and then find the file's location.
- Choose the desired file format from the drop-down list in the file type box (formerly called Projects).

The file formats from which Project can import data are seen by scrolling through the file type box. You can import data from programs that can save data in any of these file formats into Project.

- To launch the Import Wizard, select the desired file and click Open. This wizard walks you through the process of importing structured data into Project from another format.

- Click Finish after completing the Import Wizard's stages. The data is imported by the project. To open files in other formats, modify your legacy file format settings

CRUCIAL

Only when working with old file formats that you are certain are from a reliable source do you need to change your legacy file format settings. A Group Policy or other setting in your company may prevent you from changing your legacy file format setting in the Trust Center as explained here.

- To enter the Project Options dialog box, click Options after selecting the File tab in Project to bring up the Backstage view.
- Press on Trust Center.
- To access the Trust Center dialog box, click Trust Center Settings.
- Select Legacy Formats. Under Legacy Formats, choose the option you desire.
- To manage how Project should react when you try to open or save files in other formats, use the Legacy Formats page in the Trust Center dialog box.

- To exit the Trust Center dialog box, click OK. To exit the Project Options dialog box, click OK once more.

SAVE PROJECT FILES IN DIFFERENT FORMATS

For one-time or uncommon purposes, pasting Project data into other programs as explained in a previous subject might be acceptable; but, if you need to export a lot of data from Project, this method might not be as effective. Alternatively, Project data can be saved in many file formats. There are several ways to do this, including the following: For structured data interchange with other applications that accept XML, you can save the complete project in Extensible Markup Language (XML) format. Only the data you designate can be saved in a different format. Excel workbooks and text that is tab- or comma-delimited are among the supported formats. When saving to these formats, you select the desired format, select an existing export map (or make your own), and export the information.

ADVICE

The active view can also be saved to an archival format, such PDF or XPS, which maintains formatting and layout but is typically not editable.

It doesn't matter whether view is open in Project when you need to export data to a different file format. The data that can or cannot be exported is unaffected by the current view.

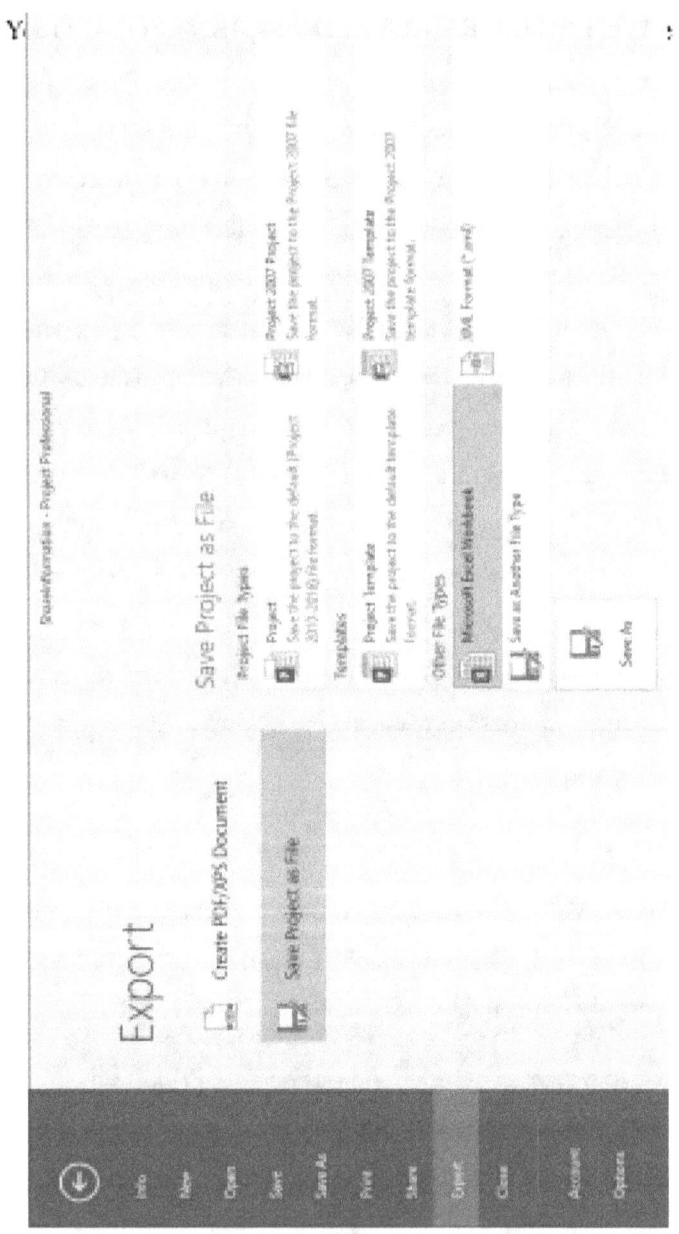

main file type categories that Project supports. Project exports the plan's data right away if you choose one of the Project formats or the XML format. Data maps are necessary for the other file types in order to regulate the export organization of certain fields from the active plan. You navigate through the Export Wizard when you start the export process for a format that needs a data map. You can utilize a data map you've already made, establish a new one, or use one of Project's built-in data maps in this wizard.

The Export Wizard displays the precise field mapping that has to be used for the export as you proceed. On this Export Wizard page, you can see and modify the field mapping specifics of a particular data map after you've chosen it. Although Project has several built-in data maps, you can create your own if they don't work for you. When you need to regularly export significant amounts of Project data to feed into different platforms or programs, data map-based exporting is very helpful.

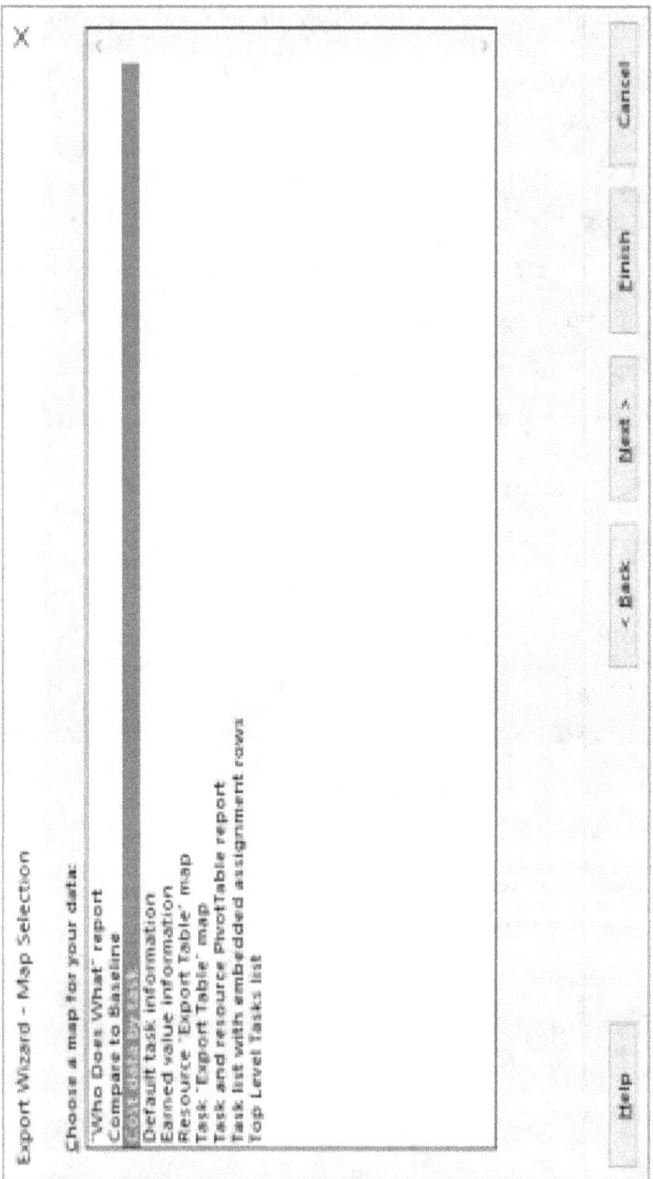

DISTRIBUTE A RESOURCE POOL AMONG SEVERAL PLANS

You may need to assign work resources (people and equipment) to more than one project at a time when managing several projects. Coordinating the time of labor resources across several projects could become challenging, particularly if they are overseen by various individuals. For instance, a resource may be assigned tasks in three concurrently running projects. The resource may be entirely or even partially assigned in each plan. Nevertheless, if you combine all of the activities from these plans for that resource, you may find that the resource has been overallocated, meaning that they have been given more work than they can manage at once.

You can observe how resources are used across several plans by using a resource pool. The resource pool is a plan that provides the resource information for other plans. It includes details on the task assignments for every resource from every plan connected to the resource pool. Work resources are not the only purpose for a resource pool. When working with cost resources across many plans, you may wish to view both the total costs across plans as well as the cost per plan in question. Similarly, you can view the total amount of material resources consumed in each unit of consumption when working with material resources across many plans. Sharer plans are those that are connected to the resource pool.

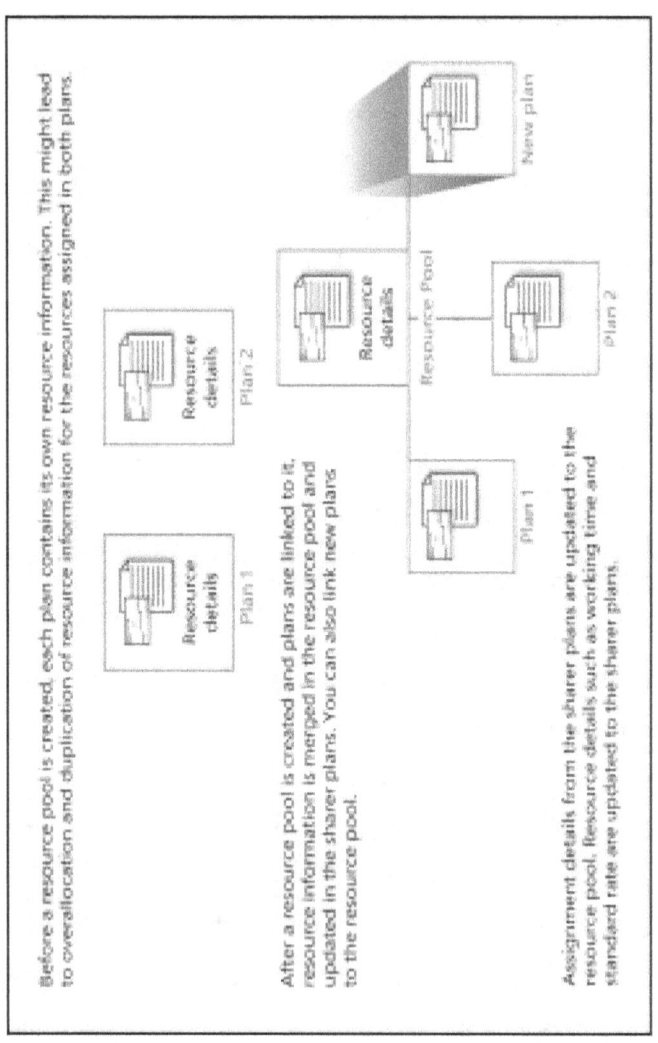

A sharer plan can be linked to a resource pool at any point in time, including when tasks are first entered into the plan, after resources are assigned to tasks, or even after work has started. It may be useful to create all-new plans sharer plans after you have established a resource pool. Making new plans as resource pool sharer plans has the time-saving benefit of making your resource information instantly available. No resource data needs to be entered again. A resource pool is of little use to you if you are managing a single project with resources that are not utilized in other plans. However, creating a resource pool allows you to perform the following if your company oversees several projects:

Even if resources are underallocated in individual plans, look for those that are overallocated across numerous plans. See the cost and resource assignment information from several plans in one place.

Modify a base calendar's working hours in the resource pool, and all sharer plans that utilize that calendar will be updated with the changes. For instance, all sharer plans are altered if you designate specific days (like holidays) as nonworking days in the resource pool.

Here's a closer look at how a resource pool can contribute to the delivery of these advantages. Examine two plans that share some of the same task-related resources. Both plans use much of the same resources. Suppose that neither plan includes any of these resources. However, you can begin to monitor the resources' actual scope of allocations more precisely after the two plans are connected to a shared resource pool.

Based on the resource names, Project combines resource data from the sharer plans in the resource pool. All sharer plans' resource information is contained in the resource pool. The allocation of resources across several strategies is now easier to see.

When working across a network with other Project users, a resource pool is extremely helpful. Individual owners of the sharer plans (which may be stored locally or on a network server) would then share the common resource pool, which would be kept in a central location, such a network server. Plans can be become sharer plans by linking them to a resource pool file using the Share Resources dialog box.

Following the creation of the resource sharing link between the pool and the plan, the project combines the resource names from the two. All sharer plans will use the most recent information when you make changes to the resource pool's maximum units, cost rates, and nonworking time. When you open a resource pool or sharer plan, Project provides you with options because they are related. Project asks you to choose how to open a resource pool file when you open it. The resource pool is opened as read-only by default.

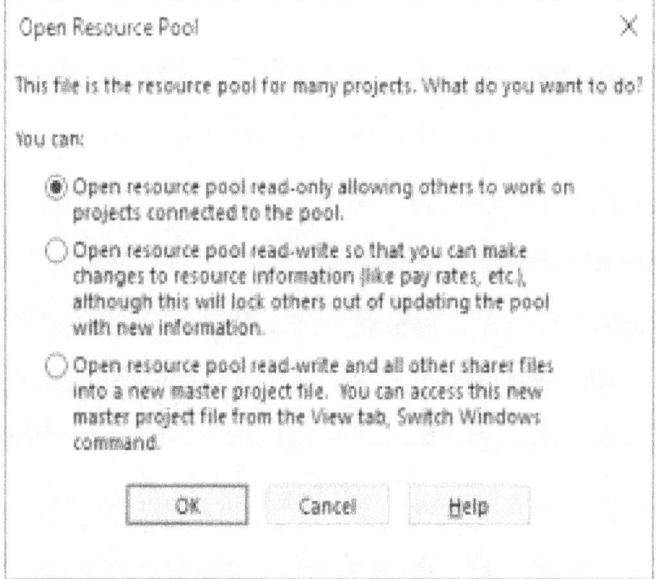

You should open the resource pool as read/write if you save it locally. If you and other Project users share a resource pool over a network, you may want to select the read-only option. You won't stop other Project users from modifying the resource pool in this manner. When necessary, you may easily push resource and assignment updates to the read-only resource pool via the sharer plan. The most recent assignment details will then be visible to anybody else who opens the resource pool. When working with resource pools and sharer plans, you must open the resource pool when you open a sharer plan in order for the sharer plan to be updated with the most recent resource pool modifications. Assume, for instance, that you modify the resource pool project calendar's working hours, save it, and then close it. The changed project calendar's working hours will not be reflected in a sharer plan that you open later without first opening the resource pool.

As previously said, one of the most significant advantages of utilizing a resource pool is that it makes it possible to observe how resources are distributed among plans. Displaying the Resource Form alongside the Resource Usage view in the resource pool is an excellent method to look at the specifics of resource assignments and allocations. When employing a resource pool, the Resource Form displays assignments across several plans. All of the resources in the resource pool and their assignments are displayed in the upper pane of this combination view, while the details of the chosen resource from each sharer plan are shown in the lower pane. One way to view the specifics of individual assignments from sharer plans is using the Resource Form. The Resource Usage view's table section can also have the Project or Task Summary Name field added. By doing this, you may see the summary task name and the project from which each work assignment is taken. Project maintains resource pool synchronization while you operate in a sharer plan, provided the resource pool remains open.

Any modifications you make to resource assignments or other resource details in one sharer plan instantly affect the resource pool and all other open sharer plans.

LINKING A PLAN TO A POOL OF RESOURCES

- Either open an already-existing resource pool or develop a fresh strategy that will serve as one. Whenever requested, open an existing resource pool as read/write.

CRUCIAL

Project asks you to choose how you wish to open a resource pool file that is connected to sharer plans. The resource pool is opened as read-only by default.

- To create a sharer plan, open or switch to the desired plan.
- Click the Assignments group's Resource Pool on the Resource tab, and then click Share Resources to bring up the Share Resources dialog box.
- Choose Use resources under Resources for "file name."
- The open layouts that can serve as resource pools are listed in the From box. In the Click the resource pool file name from the box.
- Indicate how Project should handle contradictory information if the resource name appears in both the resource pool and the sharer plan. Make sure that Pool takes precedence is chosen under On conflict with calendar or resource information if you want Project to use resource information from the resource pool instead of the sharer plan.
- To exit the Share Resources dialog box, click OK.
- Preserve the resource pool and the sharer plan.

HOW TO DISCONNECT A RESOURCE POOL FROM A SHARER PLAN

- Make the resource pool read/write accessible.

- On the Resources tab of the sharer plan, select Resource Pool. Next, select Share Resources.
- Choose Use Own Resources under Resources For "Current Project Name."
- Press OK.
- Preserve the resource pool and the unlinked plan.

HOW TO CHANGE A SHARER PLAN'S READ-ONLY RESOURCE POOL

- Make any necessary resource or assignment modifications in the sharer plan.
- In the Assignments group on the Resource tab, select Resource Pool. Next, select Update Resource Pool. The project saves the resource pool after updating the assignment details with the new information from the sharer plan. The modified assignment details will be visible to anyone else who opens or refreshes the resource pool at this time.

To see the resource pool's resource use details.

- The resource pool file can be opened or switched to.
- Click Resource Usage in the Resource Views group on the View tab to show the picture of resource usage.

- The Resource Form can also be shown in split view if you'd like. On the Scene tab, select Details under the Split View group.

HOW TO OVERSEE RESOURCE POOL-CONNECTED SHARER PLANS

- Sharer plans and the resource pool should be opened as read/write.
- Click the Assignments group's Resource Pool on the Resource tab, and then click Share Resources to bring up the Share Resources dialog box.
- Choose a sharer plan under Sharing Links. After that, you can change the conflict resolution setting, disconnect the sharer plan from the resource pool, or open that sharer plan.
- Click OK in the Share Resources dialog box when you're finished.

ADVICE

The assignment details for a sharer plan are stored in its resource pool. The assignment information for a sharer plan stays in the resource pool even if it is destroyed. You must break the link to the sharer plan in order to remove this assignment information from the resource pool. Open the resource pool as read/write to accomplish this. select

Resource Pool, then select Share Resources under the Assignments group on the Resource tab. Click the name of the now-deleted sharer plan in the Share Resources dialog box, then select Break Link. Keep in mind that a resource pool's Share Resources dialog box has different contents than a sharer plan's.

HOW TO ADJUST THE WORKING HOURS FOR EACH SHARER PLAN IN A RESOURCE POOL

- The resource pool can be opened or switched to.
- Click Change Working Time in the Properties group on the Project tab to bring up the Change Working Time dialog box.
- Choose Standard (Project Calendar) from the selection in the For calendar box.

In the For Calendar box, base calendars like Standard, Night Shift, and 24 Hours show up at the top of the list. The names of the resource calendars are displayed beneath the base calendars. All plans that are resource pool sharer plans are impacted by changes to the standard base calendar's working hours.

- Adjust your working time on the Change Working Time dialog box's Exceptions tab.

- To exit the Change Working Time dialog box, click OK. Every strategy that is shared

This modification will be reflected in this base calendar for plans of the same resource pool.

CRUCIAL

All sharer plans share the same base calendars by default, and any modifications you make to one sharer plan's base calendar are mirrored in all other sharer plans via the resource pool. Change the basis calendar that the sharer plan uses if you want to utilize different base calendar working hours for a particular sharer plan.

COMBINE PLANS

You may be in charge of several plans that share some resources and may be connected to the same organization's overarching objective or output. Coordinating with several individuals working on tasks at different times, sometimes in different locations, and often for different supervisors may even be necessary. You may need to create a single "all-up" view of different but connected plans in either scenario. Using a consolidated plan is a useful method to bring disparate project information together. This plan has other plans inside of it, known as inserted plans. Instead of existing inside the consolidated plan, the inserted plans are connected to it so that they can be seen and modified independently or from within the consolidated plan. The new data is reflected in the consolidated plan the next time it is opened if an inserted plan is modified outside of it.

Although this chapter utilizes the words consolidated and inserted plans, inserted plans are also referred to as subprojects and consolidated plans are also known as consolidated projects or master projects. Consolidated plans are an effective tool.

Consolidated plans can be useful for the following purposes:

View every task from your company's plans in one place. Report information to management at higher levels. For instance, you may incorporate a team's plan into the consolidated plan of the bigger department, which would subsequently be incorporated into the consolidated plan of the broader company. Sort your project data into several plans according to the component, phase, location, or other aspects of your project. For a thorough examination of the entire plan, you can then compile the data into a single plan. View all of the data related to your plans in one place, allowing you to group, filter, and sort the information. How does it operate, then? The Insert Subproject command

and Project's outlining tools are used in consolidated designs. At first, an inserted plan shows up as a compressed summary task in the integrated plan, with a gray summary Gantt chart. In the Indicators column, Project shows the project icon that was added.

The Gantt bars of the inserted plans are compressed in this view of a combined plan. The inserted plans are represented by summary tasks that are consecutively numbered 1, 2, and so forth. The task IDs inside each inserted plan begin at 1 when you expand the collapsed summary task of each added plan. Whether you use it as an inserted plan that you open from within a consolidated plan or as a stand-alone plan that you open directly in Project, this numbering method maintains the task IDs within each inserted plan.

The project summary task is particularly helpful when dealing with a consolidated plan. The project summary task summarizes the values from quantifiable variables like work and cost, as you may remember from Chapter 4, "Build a task list." The roll-up values for the project summary task in a consolidated plan are the sum of the values from all of the inserted plans. In the same way, the project summary task's start and end dates correspond to the earliest and latest start and completion dates found in the supplied plans.

The rolled-up values of the inputted plans are represented by the values of this summary task, including duration and work.

Connect the inserted plans to a shared resource pool as outlined in the preceding item if you wish to share resources among the inserted plans in a consolidated plan.

HOW TO DEVELOP A COHESIVE STRATEGY

- To access the Backstage view, select the File tab and then select New.
- Select the Blank project option on the New page. A new plan is created by the project. Other plans can be inserted into this plan, which will become the consolidated plan.
- Click Subproject in the Insert group on the Project tab to bring up the Insert Project dialog box.

If the plans to be inserted are in the same folder, you can add two or more plans to the consolidated plan. Press the Ctrl key to pick each plan in the Insert Project dialog box, and then click Insert.

- Click Insert after finding and selecting each plan you wish to include in the combined plan. The project adds the plan—or plans—to the overall plan. With an inserted project indicator in the Indicators column, each entered plan shows up as a collapsed summary task.

A consolidated plan that incorporates any or all of the open plans can be made rapidly. Click New Window in the Windows group on the View tab. Click OK after selecting the plans to be added to the new consolidated plan under Projects and using the Ctrl key.

HOW TO SHOW AN INSERTED PLAN'S DETAILS

- Use a task-oriented view with a table to display the combined plan, like the Gantt chart view with entry table.
- In the table's upper-left corner, click the Select All button.
- Click Outline in the Data group on the View tab, and then click All Subtasks. The inserted plan or plans are expanded by the project.

Or

- Present the combined plan in a task-oriented view with a table.

- For each inserted plan, click the expand/collapse arrow next to its name.

HOW TO SHOW THE AGGREGATED PLAN'S PROJECT SUMMARY TASK

- Click Project Summary Task in the Show/Hide group on the Format tab of the consolidated plan.

CHAPTER FOURTEEN
ESTABLISH INTERDEPENDENCE BETWEEN PLANS

The majority of projects don't just happen. One project's tasks or phases may be dependent on those of other projects. By connecting tasks across plans, you may demonstrate these dependencies. You may need to establish dependencies between plans for the following reasons:

- One plan task's completion may make it possible for another plan task to begin. For instance, before you can begin building a structure, another project manager may need to finish an environmental impact statement.

- One plan has a logical dependency on the other, even if these two tasks are managed in different plans (perhaps because they are being completed by different divisions of a construction organization). It may be necessary to postpone the commencement of a work in one plan until a resource, such as a person or piece of equipment, has finished a task in another plan. The demand for that resource may be the only similarity between the two tasks. By adding details about the predecessor work to the plan that includes the successor task, you can establish a relationship between plans. In the task's predecessor field, such as the Predecessors column in the Entry table or the ID field in the Task Information dialog box, on the Predecessors tab, you specifically insert the external predecessor link in the format File Name\Task ID.

Enter the predecessor task's file name and task number in the successor task's Predecessors box to create cross-plan linkages. Once a task relationship between plans has been established, it resembles links between tasks inside a plan. Gantt charts with gray task titles for external predecessor and successor tasks serve as a visual cue that there is a task relationship between plans. Sometimes, these are called **"ghost tasks."** In the associated file, the external predecessor manifests as a gray **"ghost task."** The source plan, which includes the predecessor task, and the destination plan, which includes the successor work, both use the same visual representation of external links.

In the file to which it is linked, the external successor task also shows up as a gray **"ghost task."** Until you break it, the connection between the two plans will stay in place. The equivalent task or external task in the other plan is deleted when a task in the source plan or an external task in the destination plan is deleted. Links between two inserted plans work similarly to regular task links within a single plan when you are dealing with consolidated plans (see the previous item). In actuality, a consolidated plan makes it simple to create cross-plan links. It may be simpler to combine the plans into a single plan and then make the necessary links if your cross-plan link requirements are complicated.

Here are some more pointers and recommendations for using cross-plan links:

- Project shows a ScreenTip with information about the external task, including the complete path to the external plan where the external predecessor task is located, when you point to the external task's Gantt bar. If you'd like, you can disable the external task display.
- Click the File tab and select Options to accomplish this. Clear the Show External Successors and Show External Predecessors check boxes in the Project Options dialog box's

Advanced tab under Cross Project Linking Options For.

- Project asks you to update the cross-plan links whenever you open a plan that contains them. If you would like not to be notified, you can either instruct Project to automatically accept updated data from the associated plan or suppress this message.
- Click the File tab and select Options to accomplish this. Choose the desired options under Cross Project Linking Options For on the Advanced tab of the Project Options dialog box.

HOW TO ESTABLISH CONNECTIONS BETWEEN TWO PLANS

- To join the two plans, open them.
- If the Entry table isn't already visible, show it in the plan that includes the task you want to be the successor task.
- To designate a task as the successor, click the Predecessors column.
- Type the predecessor task's file name and task ID (in the format File Name\Task ID) in the Predecessors field, then hit Enter.

HOW TO ESTABLISH CROSS-PLAN CONNECTIONS BETWEEN PLANS THAT HAVE BEEN ADDED TO A CONSOLIDATED PLAN

- First, choose the task that should be the predecessor, and then choose the work that should be the successor.
- Click Link The Selected Tasks in the Schedule group on the Task tab. There is a finish-to-start relationship between the two tasks.

HOW TO MODIFY A CROSS-PROJECT LINK'S RELATIONSHIP TYPE IN A CONSOLIDATED PLAN

- Decide on the next task.
- Click Information in the Properties group on the Task tab to bring up the Task Information dialog box.
- Select the tab for Predecessors.
- Select the desired link type in the Type area.

In order to remove a cross-plan link:

- First, click the successor task.
- Click Information in the Properties group on the Task tab to access the Task Dialog box for information.
- Select the tab for Predecessors.
- Choose the ID of the external task link in the Predecessors box, then click Delete.

HOW TO RECOGNIZE AND OVERSEE EACH LINK IN A PLAN, INCLUDING EXTERNAL PREDECESSORS AND EXTERNAL SUCCESSORS

- Click Links Between Projects in the Properties group on the Project tab to bring up the Links Between Projects dialog box.
- Click Close after selecting your preferred settings on the External Successors and External Predecessors tabs.
- Distribute a resource pool among several plans. The situation: You regularly allocate work resources (people) to various projects in various plans at Publishing. When all of their work throughout the plans is taken into consideration, you have sometimes unintentionally overlocated some resources, even though you control those plans in Project.
- You make the decision to establish a resource pool and link it to your present goals in order to help prevent this issue in the future. After launching the ShareResourcesA and ShareResourcesB plans in Project, carry out the subsequent actions: First, draft a fresh strategy and store it in the practice file folder. BookLove Resource Pool is the file name.

- Create the sharer plans for ShareResourcesA and ShareResourcesB pool of resources.
- In the resource pool, show the Resource Sheet view. This is how your resource pool should appear.
- Save and end all plans.

COMBINE PLANS

The situation: There are times when you have to examine data that is dispersed across several closely related but separate projects. You choose to combine them into a single plan in order to obtain a "all-up" perspective of all plans. Complete the following tasks in Project:

- First, draft a fresh strategy and store it in the practice file folder. BookLove Consolidated Plan is the file name.
- Update the BookLove Consolidated Plan using the ConsolidatePlansA and ConsolidatePlansB plans.
- To view the details of the two inserted plans, expand them in the BookLove Consolidated Plan.
- Show the task for the project overview.

ESTABLISH INTERDEPENDENCE BETWEEN PLANS SITUATION

The situation: You have determined that a task from one plan must be completed before starting a task from another plan. You choose to connect these two plans through a cross-project link. Proceed with the following tasks in the BookLove Consolidated Plan that you already created: Make task 12 in the forerunner of task 13 in ConsolidatePlansB in the BookLove Consolidated Plan.

- Save all plans and close them.

A BRIEF PROJECT MANAGEMENT COURSE

We've provided tips on how to use Project effectively while adhering to good project management techniques throughout this book. Regardless of the software tools you may employ to assist with project management, this appendix concentrates on the fundamentals of project management. The project triangle model is the main emphasis of this appendix, despite the fact that project management is a wide and intricate topic. This model takes into account the scope, cost, and duration of projects.

Recognize what makes a project. When you want to be a successful project manager, you must finish your projects on schedule, under budget, and with satisfied clients. That may seem easy enough, but how many projects have you heard of—or worked on—that were unsatisfactory to their clients, finished late, or cost excessively?

A project is temporary, to start. Every project has an end date, regardless of how long it takes—it could be a week or years. When the project starts, you might not be aware of the completion date, but it will happen eventually. Despite their many similarities, projects and continuing operations are not the same thing. As the name implies, ongoing activities don't have an end date; they continue indefinitely. The majority of the accounting and human resources departments' operations serve as examples. Project managers may also oversee continuing activities; for instance, a manager of a major organization's human resources department may organize a college recruitment fair. However, projects have a projected completion date, like the recruiting fair date, which sets them apart from continuing activities.

Then a project is an undertaking. To accomplish work, resources like people and equipment are required. Projects give a sense of being deliberate, planned occurrences since they are carried out by a team or organization. A certain level of planning and preparation is necessary before a project can be successful.

Lastly, each initiative produces a distinct good or service. This is the project's deliverable and the rationale behind its undertaking. A refinery that makes gasoline doesn't create anything special. In this instance, the goal is to provide a uniform product; generally speaking, you don't want to purchase gas from one station that differs greatly from gas at another station. In contrast, commercial aircraft are distinctive goods. Although most of us may think that all Boeing 787 Dreamliner aircraft have a similar appearance, each one is actually carefully personalized to meet the specifications of the buyer. You may already be aware that a large portion of the work that is done in the world is project-oriented. Even if project management isn't your task title, it may account for a significant amount of your work. Although project management has been acknowledged as a profession for many years, complex work has been done in some form for as long as people have been doing it. in some point during the construction of the Great Pyramids in Giza, Egypt, someone was keeping track of materials, plans, and specifications.

Nowadays, most industries acknowledge project management as a career. Examine projects according to their **scope, cost,** and **time.** There are other ways to depict project work, but our preferred approach is the triangle of triple constraints, sometimes known as the project triangle.

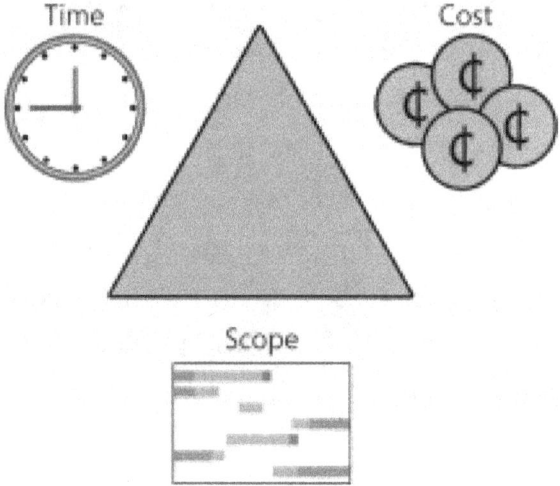

Although there are numerous variations on this theme, the fundamental idea is that every project has some sort of budget, time constraints, and labor requirements. (In other words, its scope is clearly defined.) We're employing the more generic definition of "a limiting factor" here, although the term "constraint" has a specific meaning in Project. Let's examine each of these limitations separately.

DURATION/TIME

Have you ever been involved in a project with a due date? (Perhaps we ought to inquire if you have ever worked on a project without a due date.) The one project limitation that we are all most likely most familiar with is time constraints. Ask your team members to identify the project deadline if you are currently working on one. Although they may not be fully aware of the project budget or scope, it is likely that they are all aware of their immediate deadlines and, most likely, the project's ultimate deadline.

Here are some instances of time constraints:

You have to complete the roof on your house before the rainy season starts. For a trade exhibition that begins in two months, you are putting together a sizable display stand. By the beginning of the following fiscal year, the new inventory-tracking system you are creating needs to be tested and operational. We have been taught to comprehend time since we were young. We keep time management tools with us, such as smartphones, paper organizers, and wristwatches. The most crucial limitation to control in many projects that result in a product or event is time.

THE PRICE / COST

Cost may be thought of only in terms of money, but when it comes to projects, it has a more comprehensive connotation that encompasses all of the resources needed to complete the project. The materials being used, the personnel and tools performing the work, and all other incidents and problems requiring funds or someone's time during a project are all included in the costs.

Examples of cost restrictions include the following:

You agreed to create an e-commerce website for a client at a set price. Your customer is unlikely to agree to renegotiate the contract if your costs are higher than the agreed upon price. You have been instructed by your organization's president to do a customer research project with just the personnel and tools in your department. A $3,000 grant was given to you to make a piece of public art. You don't have any other money. Cost is ultimately a limiting factor for almost all projects; very few can exceed their budget without eventually needing to take remedial action.

SCOPE / RANGE

The scope of the project and the scope of the product are two factors to take into account. A unique product—a material good or service—is the result of every endeavor that is successful. Consumers typically have preconceived notions about the characteristics and capabilities of the goods they are considering buying. The expected quality, characteristics, and functions of the product are described in great depth by the product scope. Product specs are occasionally documents that list this information. A service or event typically has certain expected traits as well. Everyone has preconceived notions about what to expect from a sporting event, concert, or party.

The effort necessary to deliver a product or service with the intended product scope is referred to as the project scope. Phases and tasks are typically used to measure the scope of a project.

Examples of scope limits include the following:

Your company was awarded a contract to create an automobile product with precise specifications, such as physical measurements of 0.02 millimeters. Project scope planning will be impacted by this product scope limitation. The lot on which you are building has a 60-foot height restriction.

Only internal services can be used to produce a portion of your product, and those services apply a different product development technique than you had intended.

The scope of a project and a product are closely related. In addition to managing the project scope, the project manager should be able to communicate with people who are familiar with the product scope.

TIME, MONEY, AND SCOPE: CONTROL PROJECT LIMITATIONS

When you have to balance the time, money, and scope limits of your initiatives, project management becomes really intriguing. Because the triangle's three sides are interconnected and altering one side has an impact on at least one other side, the project triangle serves as an example of how to balance limitations. Examples of constraint balance are given in the sections that follow.

You're running out of time. You may need to increase your budget (cost) if your project schedule's duration (time) reduces since you will need to hire more people to do the same task in less time. The scope may need to be reduced if the budget cannot be increased because the available resources will not allow you to finish all of the planned work in the allotted time. If you don't have as much time as you anticipated, you may need to reduce scope or raise expense (or both).

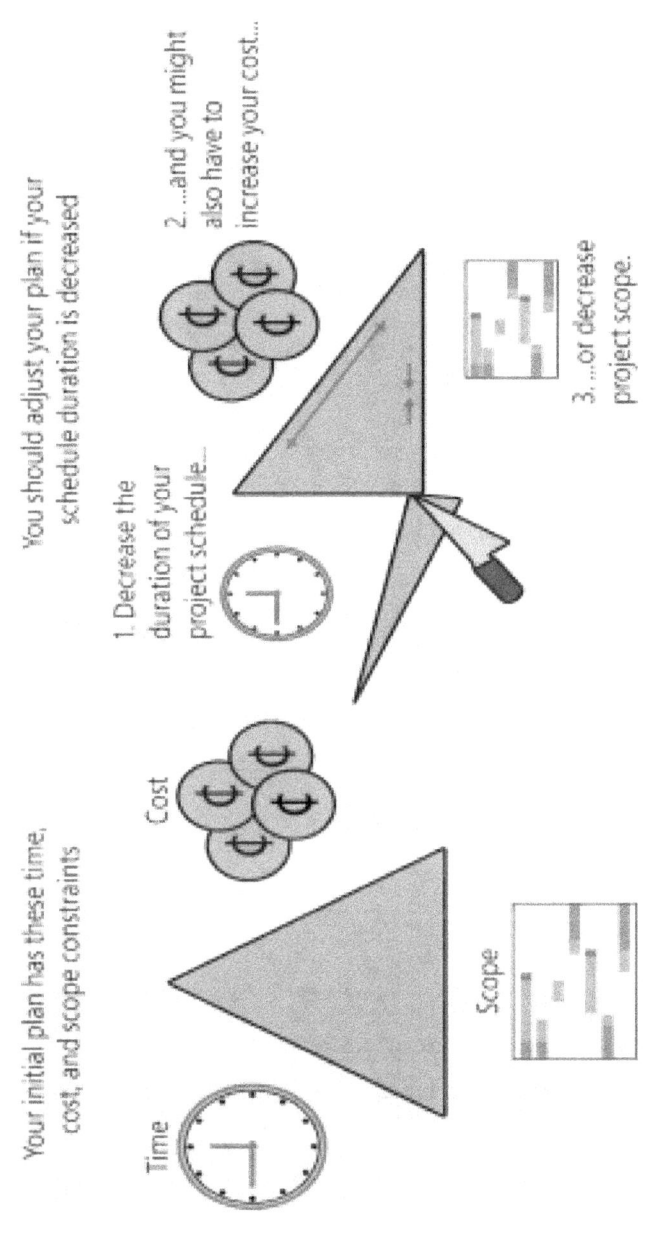

If you must shorten a project's duration, be careful not to inadvertently reduce the project's overall quality. Testing and quality control, for instance, are frequently the final tasks completed in software development projects; if project time is shortened toward the end of the project, those tasks may be the ones to be trimmed. The advantages of shortening the project's time must be balanced against the possible drawback of a lower-quality outcome.

YOUR RESOURCES ARE LIMITED

You may require extra time if your project's budget (cost) drops since you won't be able to afford as many resources or resources with the same level of efficiency. Because fewer resources cannot finish all of the planned work in the remaining time, you may need to cut the project scope if you are unable to extend the time. You may need to increase time or decrease scope (or both) if your budget turns out to be lower than you anticipated.

The grades of the material supply you had budgeted for could be examined if you need to reduce a project's budget. A substance with a lower grade does not always have a lower quality. The material may still be of excellent quality as long as the grade is suitable for the purpose for which it is intended.

Here's an example that we can all identify with: Although there are two types of restaurant cuisine—fast food and gourmet—you may discover both high-quality and low-quality varieties. The expenses of the equipment and personnel resources you intended to use should also be considered. Can simpler tasks be performed by less experienced workers for less money? However, cutting project expenses may result in a lower-quality output. As a project manager, you have to weigh the advantages and disadvantages of cutting expenses—or, more likely, convey this information to the decision-makers.

You have more work to do. You may require more time or resources (money) to finish the extra work if the scope of your project grows. Scope creep is the term for when a project's scope expands after it has begun. It's not always a bad idea to change the scope of a project in the middle of it. For instance, you may have gained new knowledge about the nature of the task since the project started, or the environment in which your project deliverable will operate may have changed. Project scope changes are only detrimental if the project manager fails to identify and account for the new needs, which means that other constraints (such time and money) are not analyzed and, if needed, modified accordingly.

The three key components of any project are scope, cost, and time. You must be able to explain to your stakeholders how each of these three limitations affects your projects if you want to be a successful project manager. This concludes our discussion of the project triangle model. This model, like many simplistic representations of complicated issues, is helpful for learning but isn't always representative of reality.

You might see projects delivered late but at the budgeted cost or with the expected scope, or you might see projects completed on schedule and with the expected scope but at a greater cost, if real projects are always carried out as the project triangle recommends. To put it another way, you would anticipate that at least one component of the project triangle will function as intended. Unfortunately, despite strict project management monitoring, many projects are delivered late, over budget, and with significantly less functionality than anticipated. Most likely, you've taken part in a couple of these initiatives yourself. The field of project management is challenging. Project management success necessitates a unique combination of expertise in the field or industry in which a project is carried out, as well as understanding of schedule procedures and tools.

Utilize Project Management to oversee your projects. Your sound judgment will always be superior to even the greatest project management technology available. But with the correct tool, you should be able to do the following: Keep track of all you learn regarding the project's work, time, and resource needs. Showcase your project strategy using standardized, clear forms. Effectively and consistently schedule resources and tasks.

There are several ways to share project information with stakeholders. Keep the project manager in charge at all times while communicating with resources and other stakeholders. You were introduced to Project's extensive capability throughout the book's chapters. You most likely have needs that this book did not cover, and not everything in it may have applied to you. We hope this book will help you get Project off to a wonderful start!

CONCLUSION

As we wrap up this Microsoft Project tutorial book, it's essential to reflect on the journey you've taken to enhance your project management skills. Throughout this guide, we've delved deep into the key functionalities that Microsoft Project offers, empowering you to navigate the complexities of project management with confidence and precision.

We began by establishing a solid foundation, exploring the interface and understanding the core components of effective project planning. You learned how to create comprehensive project plans, set timelines, and define milestones, which are crucial for keeping your projects on track. Each chapter built upon the last, gradually introducing more advanced concepts such as resource allocation, budget management, and risk assessment.

One of the standout features of Microsoft Project is its ability to provide real-time insights into project performance. By leveraging tools like Gantt charts and dashboards, you can visualize progress and make data-driven decisions. Throughout the book, we emphasized the importance of tracking progress and adjusting plans as needed. This flexibility is key to responding to changes and ensuring that your projects meet their objectives, regardless of unforeseen challenges.

Moreover, we highlighted the importance of effective communication and collaboration within project teams. With Microsoft Project's sharing and collaboration tools, you can foster a more connected and engaged team. Remember, successful project management is not just about the tools you use; it's about how you leverage them to enhance teamwork and maintain open lines of communication. By encouraging feedback and promoting a culture of collaboration, you can drive greater engagement and ensure that all team members feel valued and informed.

As you continue to apply the techniques outlined in this book, consider the lessons learned not just as a checklist, but as principles to guide your project management approach. Embrace the challenges that come your way, and use each project as an opportunity to refine your skills and expand your knowledge. The world of project management is ever-evolving, and staying curious and adaptable will serve you well.

In addition, keep in mind the importance of continuous learning. Microsoft Project is regularly updated with new features and enhancements that can further streamline your project management processes. Make it a habit to explore these updates, participate in forums, and engage with other project management professionals. This community can be an invaluable resource as you share experiences, seek advice, and learn from others in the field.

Thank you for joining us on this informative journey through Microsoft Project. We hope this tutorial has equipped you with the tools and confidence to manage your projects effectively and efficiently. As you embark on your future projects, remember that with the right planning, execution, and adaptability, you can achieve your goals and drive successful outcomes.

Happy managing, and may your future projects be both successful and fulfilling!

www.ingramcontent.com/pod-product-compliance
Lightning Source LLC
Chambersburg PA
CBHW052140220526
45471CB00004B/1455